Concha Morgades

SILK
PAINTING

for Beginners

KÖNEMANN

Copyright © 2001 Könemann Verlagsgesellschaft mbH

Bonner Straße 126, D-50968 Cologne

Project management: Arco Editorial, S. A.

Graphic design: Arco Editorial, S. A.

With contributions by Karla de Keteleare, Nadia Faus, Mª Agustina Chueca and
Jordi Andreu i Fresquet

Original title: *Pintura decorativa sobre seda*

Copyright © 2001 for this English edition:
Könemann Verlagsgesellschaft mbH

Translation from Spanish: Gillian Wallace in association with Cambridge Publishing Management

Editor: Kay Hyman in association with Cambridge Publishing Management

Project manager: Sheila Hardie for Cambridge Publishing Management

Typesetting: Cambridge Publishing Management

Project coordination: Kristin Zeier

Production: Stefan Bramsiepe

Printing and Binding: Eurografica, Marano Vicenza

Printed in Italy

ISBN 3-8290-6100-5

10 9 8 7 6 5 4 3 2 1

Contents

It is a joy to stretch out an immaculate piece of silk, but the pleasure is even greater when colors glide gently over it, creating sensual and evocative shapes. This book explains how to spread a multitude of colors and ideas over the sensuous surface of silk. There are various ways of painting on silk, each of them requiring different materials, techniques, and processes, and although we will demonstrate the traditional methods here, the approaches taken and the pieces created go far beyond classic styles. Starting from basic knowledge of the techniques, we hope to explore every possible type of decorative painting on silk and to show how creativity and imagination make a fundamental contribution to its success.

The fascinating world of silk

The art of painting on silk is a complex operation, even more so if we bear in mind that the medium used is a precious natural material. Application of the dyes to the fabric sometimes needs to be rapid and vigorous so, in order to obtain the best results, we need to first have in-depth understanding of the technique, while we are also able to appreciate the direct contact with a living fiber: silk. This fabric breathes and expresses itself in a very special way so we can establish a dialog with it that may become a rewarding relationship. The appeal of this creative collaboration is attested to by the many artists dedicated to silk painting.

Learning the basic techniques and various complementary approaches will allow us to build up a very special rapport with the fabric and painting materials. It may seem difficult at first, since painting on silk requires a lot of practice. In due course, however, thanks in particular to the magic of steam-fixed dyes that become totally integrated with the fabric, while still respecting the characteristic luminosity and texture of silk, the results are amazingly gratifying. Stimulating the imagination in this manner then inspires further explorations in this versatile fabric coloring technique.

"We create astonishing delights vying with the colors of paradise, bringing heaven down to earth."

Concha Morgades

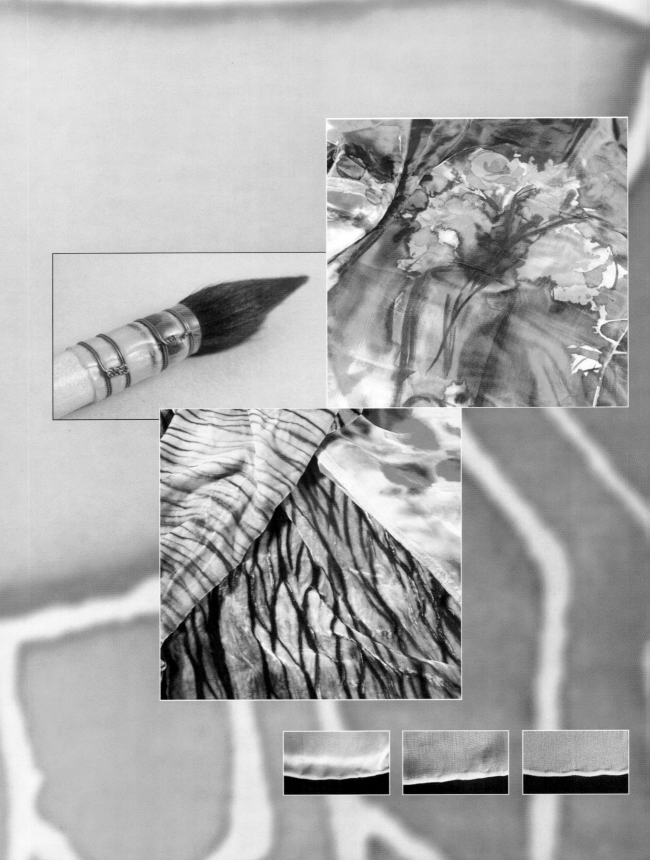

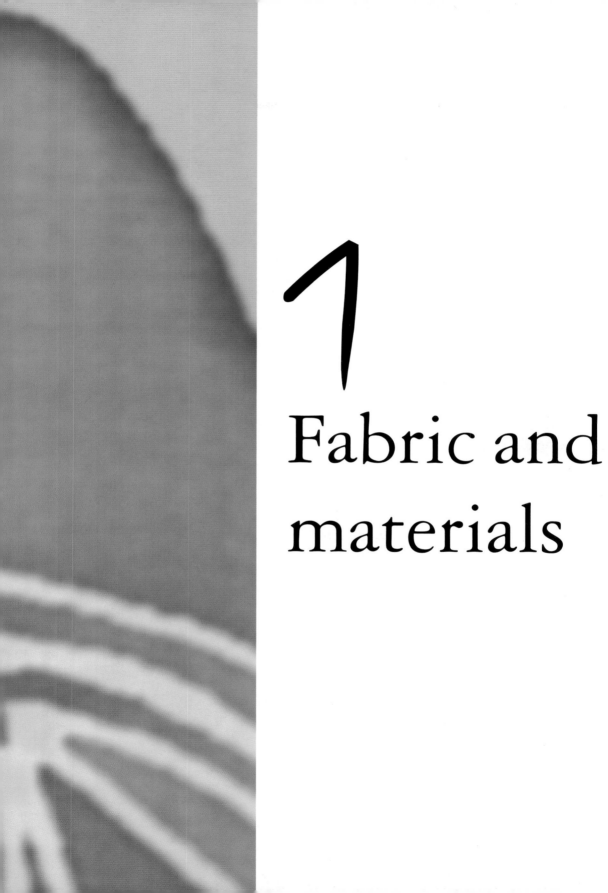

1

Fabric and materials

1.1. Silk

Fabric and materials

Depending on the warp, weft, and weight of the fabric, silk can provide a range of different draping qualities, sheen, texture, and durability. The fabrics most commonly used by silk painters are those that we list below.

Pongé is a medium- to heavy-weight fabric with a simple warp and weft; it is stiff, very close-woven, and durable, with a smooth texture. This type of silk is quite easy to obtain and is very useful for experiments and for first attempts at painting on silk. Once it has been steamed and dry-cleaned, pongé is much softer to the touch than before and its sheen improves with use.

Crepe de chine or crepe has a crinkled and elastic texture which is achieved by twisting the thread before weaving it, after which it is finished in water to reduce the coarseness of the thread and to create a crinkled surface texture. This type of silk absorbs a great quantity of dye and therefore gives colors great richness and depth. It is an ideal material for clothing.

Crinkle chiffon is a muslin type of silk but its ruched form of creasing gives a very interesting look to clothes.

Pongé

Crepe de chine or crepe

Crinkle chiffon

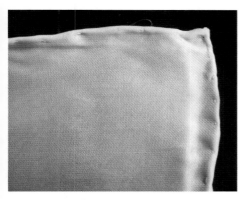

Twill is a highly resistant type of silk because it is made with a very stiff diagonal weft that is known as fluting. This fabric is very taut, although there is no danger of tearing. It is ideal for making up into lampshades, for example.

Organza is a stiff fabric but with the distinction of being rather transparent. It is normally used to make elegant items of clothing, such as wraps for formal events.

Twill

Spun silk is usually confused with unrefined silks because it has a rough texture, obvious protuberances (knops), and a dull sheen. It is the only type of silk that allows the silkworms to escape before the cocoons are gathered. The discarded short fibers from this process are woven into a rough material called floss (or noil) silk, now known as rustic silk and popular in recent years for clothing. While it is difficult to apply paint to this unrefined silk because it has not had the bast (glue-like substance) removed, a floss silk minus bast and bleached will certainly absorb dyes.

Spun silk

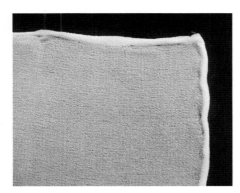

Crepe georgette

Crepe georgette is much more resistant than spun silk, but has a stiffness similar to that of crepe de chine. It drapes well and because of its special transparency and elasticity, it is suitable for a great variety of garments.

Tussore silk, also known as **wild silk**, has small knops in the thread which give it a rough texture. Problems may arise because an excess of dye can accumulate in these knops and the guttas cannot carry out their blocking function as well as in other silks. Because of its special feel, tussore silk, handled carefully, is widely used for curtains, shawls, and formal garments.

Tussore

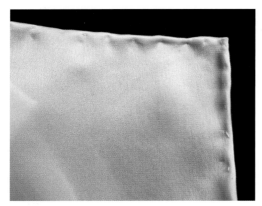
Satin crepe

Satin crepe has one shiny and one matt side. The weft and warp of this particular silk are very stiff and so it is highly suitable for making clothes and as a base for pictures.

Velvet is a type of silk with a very different feel from the other varieties. The warp and weft of the fabric pass through a machine that raises part of the fiber, then another machine cuts the fiber to a uniform level, giving the cloth a soft and special texture. An ideal style for painting velvet is very free, since the fabric does not permit the use of outliners. Painting can also be done with aerosols.

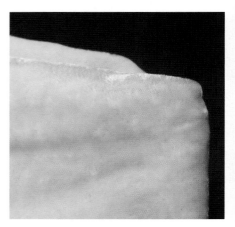
Velvet

Caring for silk

Silk is a magnificent medium: it keeps paint colors vivid and the delicacy and brilliance of its texture provides an exquisite surface. Yet silk is a practical and durable fabric that can be enjoyed for a lifetime.

Nevertheless, although silk is very resilient and hard-wearing, it is important to know how to look after it. If you wish to keep large quantities of silk, the best method is to roll it up in a cardboard tube (rather than folding it), and to put it in a cool, dry place immediately. If you wish to store it for a long time, it is best not to use plastic to wrap it up as silk is a living material and should be allowed to breathe.

Painting ready-made silk

Ideally, the decorative paint should be applied before the cloth is made up, but if you buy a ready-made item, bear in mind that care must be taken when painting near the seams. This zone is thicker and usually absorbs more dye, resulting in unwanted patches of color.

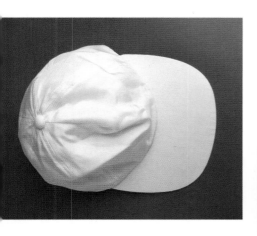

1.2. Equipment & materials

Tools

To enter the world of silk painting it is fundamental to become familiar with the equipment with which you are going to work. Once you have become familiar with the tools and processes that are explained throughout this book, you will be able to experiment more with other products and add them to your creative repertoire.

First of all, we must emphasize that the result of your painting should always be evaluated after steam-fixing which, because of the type of pigmentation contained in steam-fixed paints, gives the silk an exquisite sheen.

A finely divided ruler, adhesive tape, thick pencil, marker with invisible ink that disappears after three hours, dropper, special spray, Petit-gris paintbrush, natural sponge, and cleaning cream for ink stains.

Before starting a project, it is a good idea to be equipped with the full range of materials needed for painting on silk: a finely divided ruler, adhesive tape, a thick pencil, a marking pen with invisible ink which allows lines to be drawn on silk that disappear after three hours, a dropper to apply small doses of substances, pots with hermetic seals in which to pour the dye mixes, a special spray for fabrics with a thick weft such as spun silk, wild silk, or velvet, a Petit-gris paintbrush, a natural sponge for creating effects and backgrounds, some cotton buds, cleaning cream for ink stains, cotton rags for cleaning brushes, and plant-based paper for drawings and designs.

> ### Hint
> It is difficult to remove stains on hands created by the type of paint we use in silk painting. Instead of using bleach (which could damage the skin), rub your dry hands with cleansing cream and then wash them with water and soap.

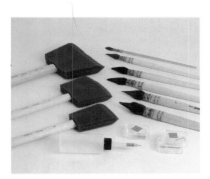

Sponges for applying the background color

To the list on the previous page, you might add scissors for cutting the silk, containers for assembling a color palette, a black marking pen for going over the lines drawn on the plant-based paper, a sheet of polyester or acetate to make a cone for applying gutta (page 19), special paintbrushes of varying sizes for painting on silk, plain straight-cut, stiff paintbrushes for the mixes made from thick substances, and finally, a gutta applicator.

Sponge

Petit-gris paintbrush. These paintbrushes are made from squirrel-hair and have the special feature of absorbing a lot of paint in the upper part while releasing a small quantity via the fine point, so the dye can be applied over a longer period of time without the need for constant replenishment. This is a high-quality paintbrush; the next one in this category is the mixed Petit-gris. It is a good idea to buy three different sizes of brush designed to cover small, medium, and large surfaces.

Petit-gris paintbrush

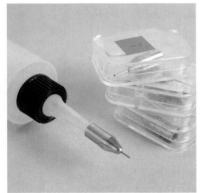

Gutta applicator

Gutta applicator with different nib sizes. The size of the aperture in the nib increases with its number. Each nib case also contains several small wires, which are used to clean the aperture. It is essential to do this every time the applicator is used.

Cotton buds

Cotton buds can be used to salvage many of the situations involving an excess of paint on the fabric.

Most of the work described in this book will be carried out on $^3/_{16}$ in. (5 mm) pongé silk as it is the most suitable type of silk for experimentation.

Preparing the cloth in the stretching frame

Preparing the silk for painting in a frame may seem to be a fairly unimportant activity, but it is absolutely crucial for achieving success with the technique you have chosen.

To begin with, the silk should be measured and cut to the required size, placed on the work surface, and stretched until it is uniform and taut.

Stretching frame

Silk stretching methods

You can buy a stretching frame, acquire rollers for stretching the fabric (available in specialist artists' shops), or even construct your own frame for stretching silk.

If you are planning a large-scale design you can build a frame using small wooden boards. It is best to use metal brackets at the corners to assemble them and then to put a pair of clamps in position to hold the frame steady.

It is also advisable to raise the frame slightly onto something solid like a pedestal if you are working on a flat surface and want to be sure the cloth will not touch the frame if it becomes loose.

Cutting the silk

In order to cut the silk in the frame we have to first make it taut. One way is to measure the length and width of silk needed, attach the edges to the inner part of the frame and stretch it lightly across, leaving a margin of just under $^3/_4$ in. (2 cm) for silk pins, tacks, or adhesive tape.

The best method, however, is to make a clean tear, because a torn piece of fabric stretches more easily and provides perfect edges and right angles.

To tear the silk you first have to attach the edges of the fabric to the frame and stretch it lightly widthwise, leaving a margin on each side, as before, for the silk pins, tacks, or adhesive tape. Make a cut of $^3/_8$ in. (1 cm) at the edge to mark the measurement and repeat the operation on the other side.

Then tear the silk along the cuts employing the same amount of force with both hands and finally, stretch the silk alternately on one side and then the other, just a few inches at a time, until the edges meet.

Another option consists of pulling a thread on one side and cutting along the line of the extracted thread.

Stretching techniques

You can use silk pins, silk hooks with rubber bands, tacks, or adhesive tape to attach the cloth to the frame.

Adhesive tape will provide a final result without leaving holes and, if you want to make geometric designs, it will also help you to maintain straight lines of gutta.

For optimum results when stretching silk fastened with adhesive tape, you must maintain a suitable temperature and humidity in your work room. If the area where you carry out this operation is very humid, it will be more difficult for the tape to stick. The tape must be masking tape, which does not leave any sticky residue on the fabric, with a minimum width of 1 in. (2.5 cm).

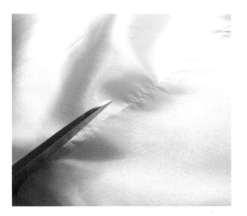

Three-point silk pins and **flat drawing pins (tacks)** make it easier to move your arm more freely when painting because they are flush with the frame.

Silk hooks secure the material to the frame and the rubber bands prevent it from becoming loose.

We must not forget that silk is a living fabric and that it adapts very easily. There is no need to be afraid of overstretching it: it is vital to make the fabric very taut so that we can achieve a good result.

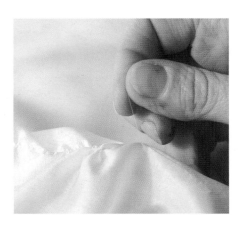

Stretching silk using adhesive masking tape

In order to carry out this operation, first cut four lengths of adhesive tape, one for each side of the frame. Position the strips of tape with the sticky side facing upwards, fastening the ends with shorter strips of tape placed sticky side down. Then, leaving half the width of the tape free, stretch the fabric onto the tape.

Stick the silk to the frame starting at the shortest end. If the piece of silk is not straight enough, you can pull it off and try again.

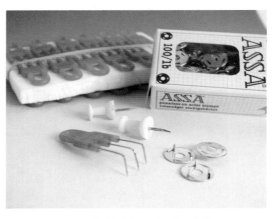

Possible fasteners for a stretching frame hooks, three-point silk pins, and map pins.

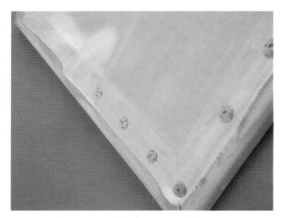

Stretching the cloth using tacks.

Stretching silk using silk pins or tacks

Place the fabric on the surface of the frame and begin to fix the silk pins or tacks at one of the corners. Continue with the remaining pins, first on the other corners of the frame, then along the sides.

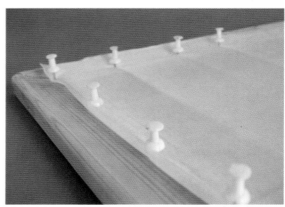

Tacks and map pins are positioned in the same way, but the latter do not give the same amount of mobility.

Stretching silk using hooks and rubber bands

First, prepare the hooks by fixing a rubber band onto the ends of each one, and then tack the rubber bands onto the frame. Next, position a few hooks at regular intervals just adjacent to each other. We will begin stretching the material by attaching one of its shorter sides to the hooks first, so we can then stretch the whole piece slowly and in the same order in which we began to fasten the silk to the hooks.

Position the hooks next to each other at regular intervals.

Dyes

The brilliance of decorated silk is achieved precisely through the dyes used. These are translucent and when applied to silk they become an integral part of the sensual fabric.

Normally we find these dyes in shops that specialize in decorative products for silk. They must not be confused with fabric paints, which contain compounds and preparations that make them appear to be opaque.

For the pieces of work that appear in this book products from the French firm Dupont are used. Considered non-toxic, these belong to the group of dyes first developed for protein-containing fibers such as wool or silk; their basic component is dye diluted in a slightly alcoholic solution.

Different iron-fixed or heat-fixed dyes.

Steam-fixed dyes for silk contain pigments that are easily absorbed by the fiber in the fabric, so they become impregnated with the color of the dye. Once this has been fixed, it produces a shimmering result as well as aiding the creation of pictorial atmosphere, without altering the nature of the silk.

In contrast, dyes that are iron-fixed or heat-fixed contain a special gum that closes the pores of the fabric so that it does not totally absorb the pigment.

Steam-fixed dyes for silk have a high concentration of pigment.

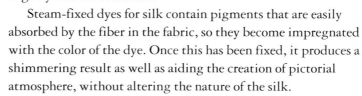

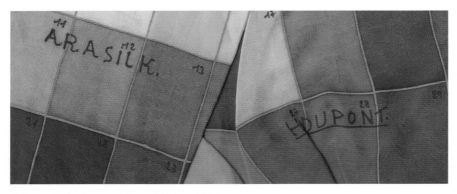

Color chart showing the range of dyes available in specialist shops.

These dyes alter the natural texture of the silk, making it stiffer, and the colors are less intense. Their advantage, however, is that, once we have completed the piece of work, the colors are easily fixed with an iron. The manufacturers recommend that dyes be stored in a cool, dark place, where they can remain in good condition for two years. If the dye thickens or accumulates in the bottom of the pot, it is a sign that it has lost its effectiveness.

When working with dyes and fabrics that reflect the light, such as silk, primary subtractive colors are used to mix all the other colors. The three most important subtractive colors are light yellow, cyan blue, and magenta.

Outliners, thickeners, and solvents

Other substances needed for decorating silk with steam-fixed dyes are thickener, Essence F, transparent gutta, antifusant, alcohol, concentrated solvent, and a special soap designed for washing silk.

Outliners

Gutta and other outlining materials are usually applied to the silk with an applicator or a cone in the form of lines. Their primary function is to control the distribution of the dye and to keep some painted surfaces away from others.

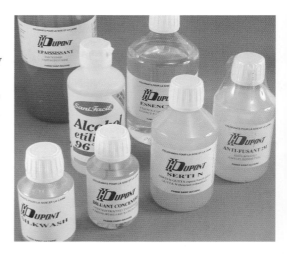

Gutta, also known as gutta-percha, is a substance consisting of a milky latex coagulant obtained from a hybrid species of *Palaquium*, a tropical tree cultivated in the plantations of Malaysia, Borneo, and Sumatra. Gutta is sold in numerous different colors and shades from basic to tertiary. This thick material is available in two forms: petrol-based or water-based.

Petrol-based gutta

This should not be too thick and must spread easily over the silk; if it does not, the fibers will not absorb it readily and the dye will seep from one surface to another. To avoid this, it is usually diluted with a few drops of Essence F, also known as the dry-cleaning fluid PER.

Once the silk has been steam-fixed and washed to eliminate the remaining pigments, this type of gutta will remain. There is, in fact, no reason for it to disappear since it usually remains integrated into the cloth. If you wish, it can be removed by dry-cleaning.

Water-based gutta

Water-based gutta is a weaker outliner so projects in which this type of substance is used will not permit many layers of color or the mixing of too many products. The advantage is that once the silk has been fixed and washed, the gutta simply disappears in water. There are three types of water-based gutta: colored, pearlized, and metallic.

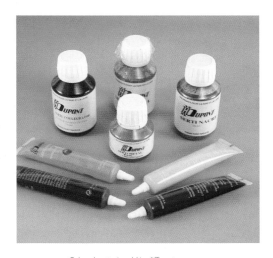

Colored gutta is sold in different shades, from basic to secondary or tertiary colors. Pearlized gutta is reminiscent of the brilliance and intensity of metallic paint and metallic gutta appears in gold, silver, copper, etc.

Hint

If you wish to add color to a transparent gutta, it can be mixed with colored guttas that have the same petrol component. Because the dyes are hydroalcoholics, you cannot mix them with gutta to color it.

Key materials for silk painting with iron-fixed dyes: thickener, transparent gutta, antifusant, solvent (only for iron-fixed dyes).

Antifusant

This substance treats the silk by blocking the pores of the fabric and allows you to work on the surface without the paint running too easily. It is also sold in two forms: petrol-based and water-based.

Petrol-based antifusant runs over the silk but never mixes with the dyes. When you want to clean sponges or paintbrushes that you have used to apply this substance to the silk, you should always use Essence F.

If you use antifusant, the silk will lose part of its natural fall and, when removing it from the material, the method is the same as with petrol-based gutta. It is not necessary to remove the antifusant but once it has been fixed, if you wish to do so, this can be done by submerging the silk in Essence F or by having it dry-cleaned with PER.

It is a good idea to use hard, low-quality paintbrushes to apply the antifusant to avoid using up your good brushes. Never mix antifusant with color dyes.

Thickeners

Water-based thickeners

A thickener is a vegetable gum solution that acts as a barrier and gives a gelatinous consistency to the color of paint. It is transparent but it can be mixed with dyes which give it their color and allows it to acquire a thicker consistency.

For this reason thickener is not appropriate for detailed and supple designs. It affects the silk in a rather irregular way, imparting a very individual character. Thickener allows you to create pictorial effects, glazes, or visual tricks by using a spatula. It is mixed with the water in the proportion of 25–50% to obtain a liquid similar to a slightly thin yogurt. Because of its consistency it is better to use flat, stiff paintbrushes or spatulas to spread it onto the surface of the silk.

> *Hint*
> Metallic and pearlized guttas are often used not only as outliners, but also as decorative motifs in designs. In this case, you first have to iron the silk, then have it fixed so that the gutta becomes permanent.

Thickener takes a little while to dry and normally gives the fabric a stiffness that disappears later on. After a wash, the silk returns to its natural texture. In addition, since thickener increases the density of the dyes, it can be used with silkscreen printing.

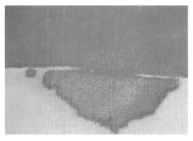

Solvent is ideal for removing marks caused by errors with steam-fixed dyes: use drops of solvent on cotton buds.

Hint

All the tools used with thickener must be cleaned with water first.

Hint

Special soaps are available to wash silk that has been fixed. These ensure that the more intense shades of color do not dye the clear edges of the fabric. If you cannot find any of these, use a few drops of vinegar instead.

Solvent

Concentrated solvent

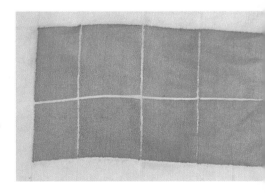

Adding solvent to the dyes makes the finished silk more brilliant and intense, while preventing it from appearing rough and dull once it has been steam-fixed.

This substance, which can be found in any dry-cleaners, is mixed with distilled water in the proportion of $1^1/_2$ fl oz (40 ml) solvent to $1^3/_4$ pints (1 liter) water, producing a fluid that can be kept for some time (though this will reduce the colors of steam-fixed dyes).

On the other hand, solvent contains a substance that helps preserve the color of the dyes and their mixtures for longer on the fabric and also allows the dyes to flow more easily over the silk. Concentrated solvent allows you to obtain nuances of color and beautiful shading effects, as well color displacement, while the displacement technique makes it possible to create such effects as transparencies, mother-of-pearl, and marbling (refer to the techniques sections later in this book).

You can also make your own solvent by mixing isopropyl alcohol and distilled water together. Alcohol is a diffusing agent that helps distribute the dye evenly over the silk. Too much alcohol can destroy the lines of gutta, so water must be added to reduce its strength.

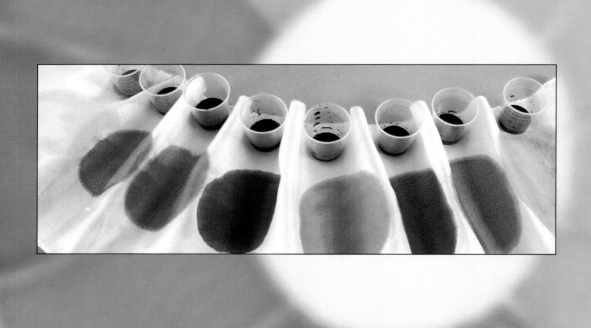

2

Silk

and color

2. Silk and color

Introduction to the theory of color

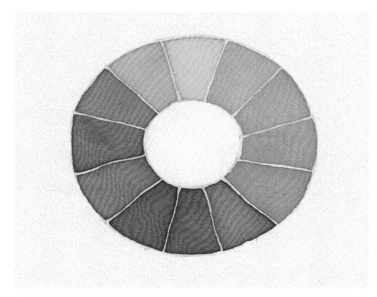

Color wheel showing the primary colors: yellow, magenta, and cyan blue; the secondary colors: violet, green, and orange; and the complementary colors.

Color is the chromatic impression that rays of light (natural or artificial) produce on our retina. It is, therefore, a combination of physical matter and of light that also has the capacity to arouse and communicate feelings.

Color is certainly an essential element in creative expression, since it can depict what is represented with total realism. However, when you talk of color you may be referring to several different concepts, because color is a subjective sensation that is received by your sense of sight, but it is also a quality belonging to objects and materials, like the dyes with which you paint.

Color is not a substance, nor is it part of the light: it is a sensation produced by the reflection of light onto matter that is transmitted through the eye to the brain. It is, therefore, a product of the mind, a subjective experience. For this experience to occur, in the first place a ray of light is needed, a physical phenomenon that can be measured and represented. In the second place, this beam of light must act on the retina, a still little understood physical and chemical reaction. Finally, the brain has to receive the signal.

24

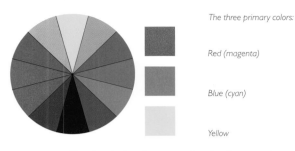

The three primary colors:

Red (magenta)

Blue (cyan)

Yellow

The color wheel used by painters is based on the systematic combination of the colors of the spectrum, starting from the three primary colors: red (magenta), yellow, and blue (cyan).

Primary colors

There are three basic colors: yellow, cyan, and magenta, known as the primary colors. These colors are the basic shades that you work with to produce mixes and to paint on silk. The primary colors cannot be obtained by mixing, although if you mix two primary colors together you will obtain the secondary colors: green (yellow through to cyan), orange (yellow through to magenta), and violet (magenta through to cyan).

Complementary colors

A primary color and the secondary color that is obtained from the mixing of the two remaining primaries form the complementary colors. So, orange is the complementary of cyan; violet of yellow, and green of magenta.

The complementary colors are also defined as those that are diametrically opposed on the color wheel.

A juxtaposition of two complementary colors creates an effect of maximum contrast via the chromatic intensity that they produce; therefore, a picture that is painted in complementary colors is said to use chromatic contrasts.

Complementary colors that are mixed with each other cancel each other out and result in a neutral gray.

Tone, value, and intensity

The human eye is capable of recognizing three measurable properties of color. Tone is the first: this is the name given to each of the principal colors of the spectrum, for example red, green, and blue.

The second recognizable property is the value, which refers to the darkness or lightness of a color when it is compared with the range of grays. Therefore, the value is the degree of luminosity that you perceive in a color. Yellow is the most luminous of all the colors,

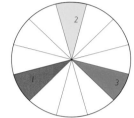

The three primary colors situated on the color wheel: magenta (1), yellow (2), and cyan (3).

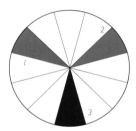

The three secondary colors situated on the color wheel: orange (1), green (2), and violet (3).

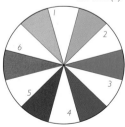

The six tertiary colors situated on the color wheel: orange yellow (1), apple green (2), greenish blue (3), purple (4), violet red (5), and red (6).

while violet is the least luminous of all. White, black, and gray are not included as they are not considered to be colors. But white can be added to a color to change the tone, so that the color is made lighter and given a higher value in the range of grays. Black can also be added and then you will obtain a color that is darker and lower down the range of grays.

The third property is the intensity: this relates to how bright or muted a color is, becoming more intense (brilliant) the nearer it is to the primary color.

Color mix

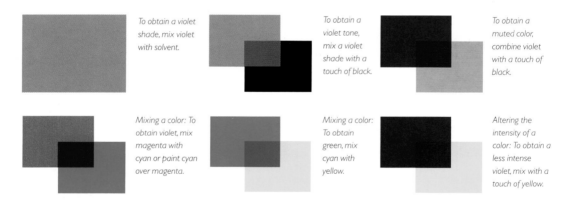

To obtain a violet shade, mix violet with solvent.

To obtain a violet tone, mix a violet shade with a touch of black.

To obtain a muted color, combine violet with a touch of black.

Mixing a color: To obtain violet, mix magenta with cyan or paint cyan over magenta.

Mixing a color: To obtain green, mix cyan with yellow.

Altering the intensity of a color: To obtain a less intense violet, mix with a touch of yellow.

There are two methods of mixing colors when working with dyes. You can mix the color first and then apply it to the silk, or you can create the color on the silk by painting in layers. Layered painting eliminates the white outliner lines and permits the gradual emergence of images and colors.

It helps to know that, whether you make prior mixes or paint in layers, you should not combine more than three colors in order to obtain a new color. In the majority of cases, a fourth color would produce a muddy shade.

When you paint in layers, you will obtain better results if you use the purest and lightest colors first and then those that are darker and deeper.

Hint

Do not apply more than two or three layers of dye to the surface of the silk because it could spoil the color.

Making a color chart

To begin with, make a little palette with the primary and secondary colors, as well as black, and pour these into glass or plastic pots. Then prepare some pongé silk on the stretching frame (pages 15–17) and collect the following materials: gutta, tape, scissors, Essence F solvent, poor-quality stiff paintbrush or wooden stick for mixing, pencil, invisible ink pen, set square, ruler, piece of paper, silk pins or tacks, plastic cup, glass cup, sheet of polyester or acetate 4×4 in. (10×10 cm).

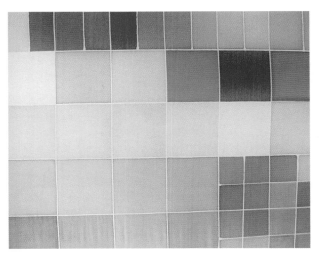

Materials needed to use gutta for making a color chart.

This is the finished color chart that you are going to make using silk in a 20 × 20 in. (51 × 51 cm) stretching frame

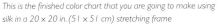

Hints

The gutta must be applied to the silk slowly and continuously; if it falls intermittently, the dye will easily seep through the fabric. If you are working with transparent gutta it is helpful to place some colored paper on the other side of the frame, so you can make sure that the line of gutta is well sealed. You can also check this by holding the frame up toward the light.

Making a gutta applicator

Using the set square, mark a 4×4 in. (10×10 cm) square with a pencil on the polyester or acetate sheet and then cut it out.

Using both hands, make a little cone leaving a small hole at the end, that is the right size to fit the point of a tack.

Pour the gutta into a glass cup (never into a plastic one because the gutta could burn it). Mix some drops of the solvent essence F into the cup of gutta. This is to dilute the gutta, since it will not penetrate the fabric easily if it is too thick and paint may then spread into other, undesired areas. Finally, stir the two substances together well with the paintbrush or stick.

Hold the cone in one hand and cover the hole with your thumb, then pour the mixture inside. Make sure you do not turn the cone upside down.

When the cone is not needed for applying the gutta, leave it supported inside a plastic cup, with the hole closed with the point of a tack.

Mark out a margin on the cloth in the stretching frame $3/8$ in. (1 cm) from the edge of the fabric, using the invisible ink pen (so the ink will later disappear).

Now place the ruler parallel to one of the edges of the stretcher with the thickest part on the inside of the stretcher.

Take the homemade gutta applicator and apply the gutta, using the edge of the ruler to help you trace the straight lines that will divide up the color chart.

The squares on the chart can start at $2^3/8 \times 2^3/8$ in. (6×6 cm) and be made smaller later. In this way divide up first a line of six squares, a second one of 12, a third of six, etc.

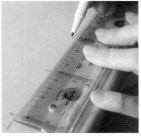

Once the squares of the color chart have been traced, you can start to paint the first strip with the primary colors plus black. So, with a suitable paintbrush, apply cyan blue, ultramarine blue, violet, magenta (or fuchsia), red, and yellow.

The second row of squares on the color chart will be painted with the secondary colors, created by mixing two primary colors from the first strip.

The third row is composed of the complementary colors: black with white, the cyan with orange, ultramarine with yellow, magenta with cyan, yellow with blue, and finally, red with green.

The fourth, fifth, and sixth rows of squares can be made up of pastel shades, so dilute the dyes and their mixes with solvent.

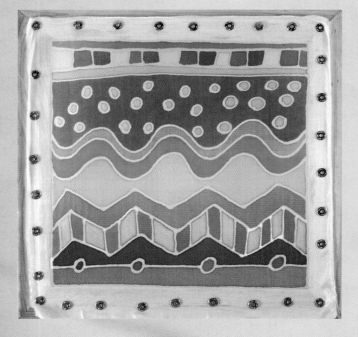

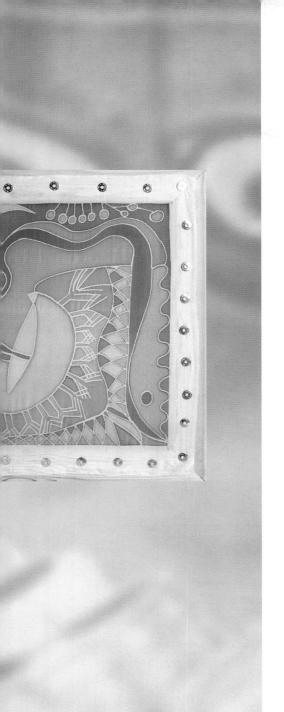

3

Basic techniques

31. Basic techniques

Knowledge of basic silk painting techniques will give you a glimpse into the fascinating world of textile printing. The lessons in this chapter focus on the use of outliners and thickeners to enable us to apply color. It is vital to understand how these coagulants work so that, to a certain extent, we can prevent dye from spreading over the whole surface and so be able to work on it in different ways.

In some examples a prior design is created on plant-based paper, but in others there is an emphasis on spontaneity, so that you need only a slight idea of what you want to accomplish and the serious work lies in experimenting and letting your creativity flow. Therefore it is important to bear in mind that the resulting pieces of work are a small sample of what can be achieved with each technique, and you can go much further if you are keen to explore other possibilities.

Practically all the pieces of work in this basic techniques chapter, and in the following complementary techniques chapter, have been carried out using pongé silk, to demonstrate that a silk fabric that is accessible and useful for experimentation can still produce good results. You must bear in mind that the colors applied to this type of silk will be much more vivid and will shine in all their splendor when the fabric has been fixed and cleaned, so you should be cautious when choosing the dyes: you could have more than one surprise.

The internal measurements of the stretching frame that you will use throughout the following examples are 12 × 12 in. (30.5 × 30.5 cm). This is a small size, but one that allows you to experiment successfully.

One step that must be repeated in each exercise, even though it is not specified continuously, is the tracing of a line of gutta as a margin around the fabric, just bordering the interior of the stretching frame. This is indispensable in order to avoid the dyes spreading toward the frame and to make sure they do not seep into the white part where the tacks are placed. In fact, in the following exercises we will stretch the silk using these, because it is an easy and economical method. You must remember, however, that the tacks have to be removed with a flat blade and that they must be completely cleaned of dye before you reuse them.

In the following exercises we will be using a range of steam-fixed dyes and and petrol-based gutta and thickener (except in certain cases where other substances are particularly specified).

It is useful to remember which products can be mixed together. Never mix any products that are not featured in the table below:

Possible combinations

Thickener + water

Thickener + dyes

Water + dyes

Petrol-based gutta + Essence F (a solvent)

Alcohol + water

Alcohol + dyes

1¹/₂ fl oz (40 ml) concentrated solvent +

1³/₄ pints (1 liter) distilled water + dyes

Working from this, you will be able to remember, for example, that all the useful products that we may use with petrol-based gutta or antifusant are cleaned with Essence F but, on the other hand, those used with thickener or dyes are simply cleaned with water alone.

One more point, which applies to each exercise where we use petrol-based gutta, is the dissolution of a few drops of Essence F into the gutta so that it becomes less dense and can be better absorbed by the silk. Essence F, a substance that you can find in any dry-cleaners, fulfills the function of dissolving products that contain petrol, such as antifusant or gutta.

Remember too that it is safer to pour products containing petrol into glass bottles because the petrol may burn plastic ones.

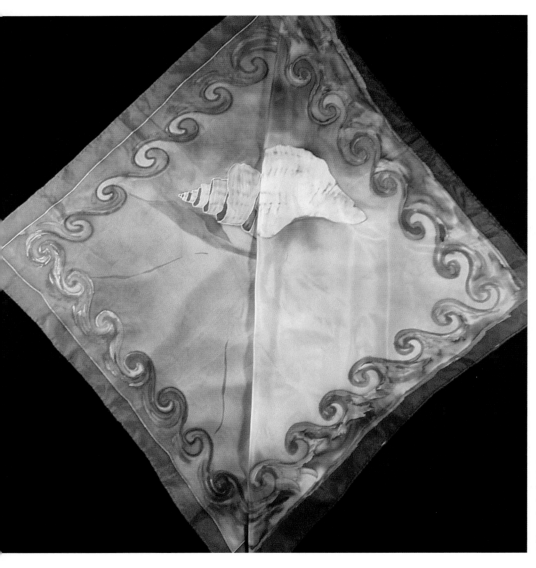

Examples of the results of fixing colors. In the area on the right, steam-fixed dyes have been used and, on the left, iron-fixed, non-steam dyes. The steam-fixed dyes give a far greater intensity of color than the iron-fixed.

Hint

To wash tacks used to stretch silk, they should be placed in a container with water and alcohol and left to soak for a few minutes. The container should then be shaken to release the dye.

Gutta application techniques

Transparent gutta

Gutta is an outliner that allows several layers of color to be applied on silk without fear that the ink will spread to another area.

Painting with dyes

Painting on silk with dyes is a wonderful and rewarding experience but not an easy one, since the silk responds differently from paper. It is therefore a good idea always to have a piece of cloth to experiment on first with any color mixes that you are thinking of incorporating into your design.

Steam-fixed dyes are usually quite concentrated and, although you can apply them directly, it is better to dilute them before use. Precisely because of their high color concentration, they may produce stains or ring marks if you paint directly from the bottle onto the thicker silks.

It has already been noted in the equipment and materials chapter that dyes dissolve in solvent. When they have dissolved, they will spread more easily over the surface of the silk.

When you proceed to painting on the silk, you do not need to slide the brushstrokes along the edge of the line of outliner; if you paint a fraction of an inch away from the outline, the dye will spread because the silk absorbs the color quickly.

It is also important not to pause during the painting of a surface and never to make another brushstroke on an area that has already been painted and has dried because water stains and other marks could appear that would be hard to eliminate.

> ### Hint
> We must remember that the paint dries more quickly in summer than in winter; so it will be easier to mix colors when the dye remains wet for a longer period of time.

1

Step by step
TRANSPARENT GUTTA

It is not a good idea to apply a gutta that is excessively thick, so dissolve some drops of Essence F into it so that it seals perfectly. But remember too that the gutta will not be able to act as a barrier if it is too liquid.

1. First, draw the design that you are going to paint on the silk on plant-based paper with a pencil and the help of a finely marked ruler.

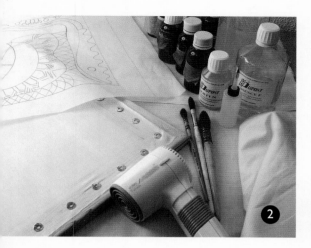

3. Begin to trace the line of gutta using the applicator. To do this, place the plant-based paper underneath the stretching frame, from where the design will show through the silk as long as the fabric is taut. You can apply the gutta by following the pencil lines.

2. Equipment and materials needed for the transparent gutta technique: steam-fixed dyes, Essence F, special paintbrushes for applying dye to silk and a flat, stiff brush for mixing the solutions, bottle of water, rags, petrol-based gutta, stretching frame and tacks, 1/4 in. (5 mm) pongé silk, plant-based paper, pencil and a hairdrier.

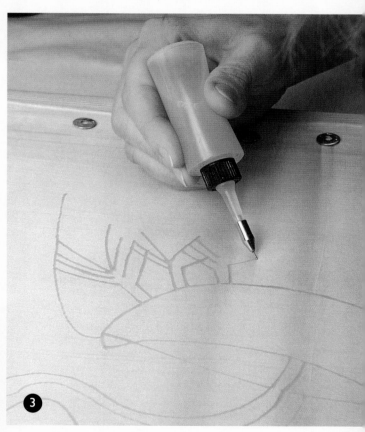

4. To check whether the seal of the gutta is perfect, bearing in mind that the lines of the outliner should completely penetrate the silk so that they can act as a barrier against the liquid dyes, study the the lines of gutta against the light. If you see areas with weak lines, go over them again with the applicator.

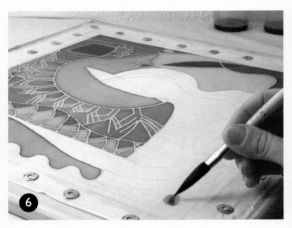

6. If you have not had any experience of applying color on a surface before, it is a good idea to decide beforehand which shades of dye to paint onto the design. Then, after making some preliminary tests on a piece of silk and mixing the dyes in different jars, you can apply the dye using the special paintbrush.

5. If you do not want to leave the gutta to dry out naturally, you can use a small hairdrier on it, then study it again against the light to see if the lines are now well sealed. Once the gutta's seal is seen to be completely dry, you can begin to paint the silk with the dyes in the spaces between the lines of gutta.

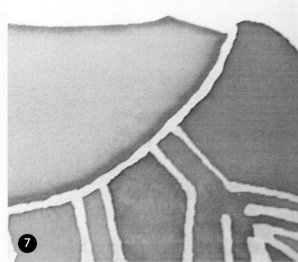

7. The secret of this technique lies precisely in the fact that the lines of transparent gutta do not allow the color to pass through from one zone to another.

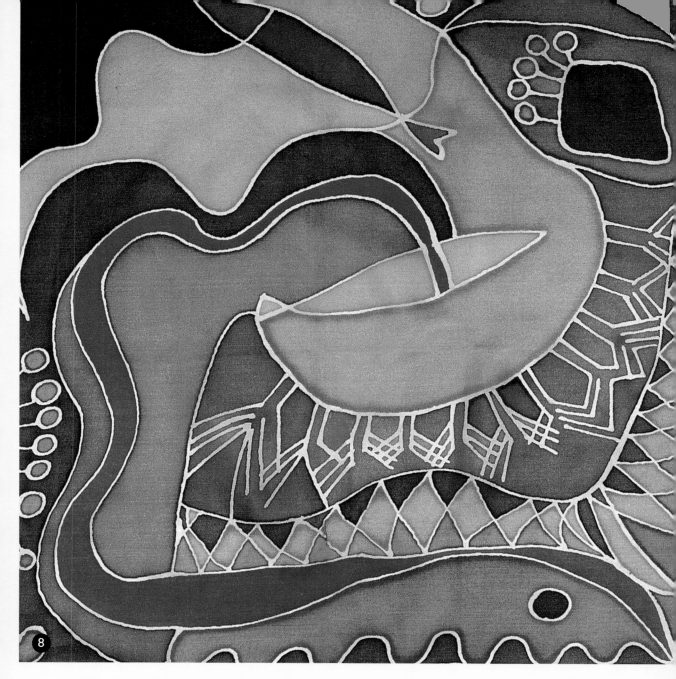

8. The final result is a design entwining earth colors, greens, and a turquoise blue, perfectly combined with the white lines of the silk, which shines through the transparent gutta. The transparent gutta will remain on the silk even after it is fixed.

Colored gutta

Superimposing gutta to create transparent color

Silk painters apply colored gutta to the silk as a background when they do not want it to be excessively translucent. They can choose from various shades of gutta available on the market, with their applicators in the form of a bottle or a tube, and these can also be mixed together to create other colors.

In the next example we will adopt a marine theme and would like the gutta to have a rather indefinite brown color in order to superimpose other shades, so it is important to make sure that its outline does not stand out too much. For this reason the brown-colored gutta will be mixed with transparent gutta. If you cannot find a brown-colored gutta you can create it by mixing red, yellow, and blue guttas.

At the end of the project we will add a metallic gold gutta, since we want to depict a net over the marine background. This gutta will not serve the function of an outliner, but instead is applied as a purely decorative material.

2 Step by step
COLORED GUTTA

Petrol-based gutta is again used in this example, but this time we will give it another color and achieve a transparent effect by applying dyes to the gutta.

Part one

1. First of all, on a piece of plant-based paper draw out the design that you are going to paint on the silk. This time we have chosen a number of shapes that remind us of a marine theme, within which we will then paint a transparent arrangement of blues and light browns.

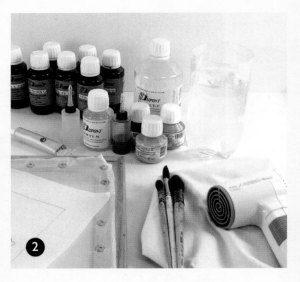

2. In order to apply this technique you will need steam-fixed dyes, transparent petrol-based gutta, Essence F (to dilute the gutta), paintbrushes, gutta applicator with 0.25 in. (0.5 mm) nib, hairdrier, bottle of water, rags, plant-based paper, colored gutta, and metallic gutta.

3. Begin to apply the colored gutta following the lines on the plant-based paper that show through the silk as before.

4. Prepare a solution of water mixed with concentrated solvent, to be added to the paints you are going to apply to create the overall background for the design.

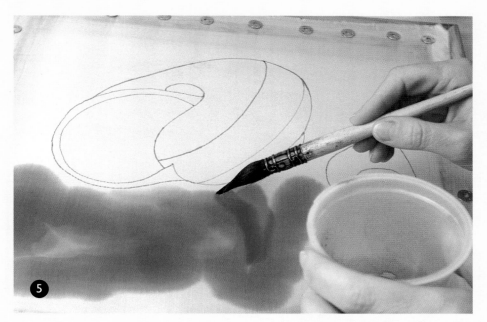

5. Start to paint the background with brush-strokes of diluted violet tones and then add a light blue to the same surface.

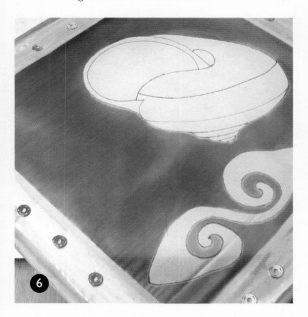

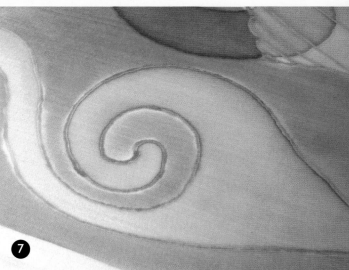

7. Paint the marine motifs that are still white with a light brown dye.

6. Finish painting the marine background with a mix of violet and diluted blue dyes so that the only surfaces left unpainted are those outlined with the colored gutta.

Part two

1. Once all the paint on the compositic
is dry, and with the design on th
plant-based paper placed underneat
the stretching frame, start to apply th
transparent gutta, tracing the line
the shapes that will be superimpose
on those that have already been drawr

2. The transparent gutta that you
have applied over the lines of the
new shapes in the composition
will now take on the color of the
background to the design.

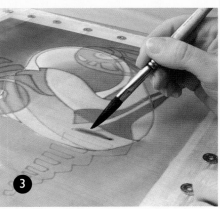

3. Once the outliner is dry, you can then begin
to paint the surfaces in a light beige color, thus
creating a transparent effect between the first
and second set of designs.

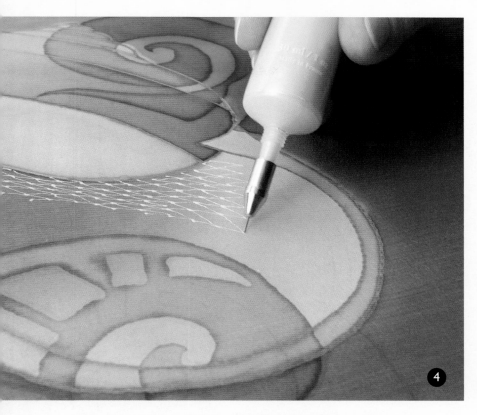

4. As a decoration, trace the lines of a net, starting from the large shell. Draw this design in metallic gold gutta, which will make the final result more attractive. In this particular example, the metallic gutta plays a purely decorative role and does not act as an outliner.

5. A detail of the finished design before the dyes have undergone the final steam-fixing process.

Correcting mistakes in applying gutta

It is very common to have difficulties when you come to trace a line of gutta. One type of problem can be caused by dragging another object along, such as the sleeve of a jersey, which causes the line to spread out and become thicker or move away from the planned design. Such a situation is easy to resolve: the best thing to do is to use a cotton bud that has been moistened in Essence F.

Pour a little quantity of Essence F into a wide-necked bottle into which you can insert the cotton bud.

After rubbing the moistened bud several times on the surface where the gutta was smudged, you will see that the gutta disappears quite easily. It is important to bear in mind that this area will be altered, however, and that, even though an outliner is reapplied, the brushstrokes of dye will not work in the same way as in other, unaffected areas. So, for example, the dye might spread more easily.

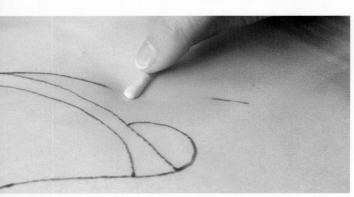

Preparing the silk with antifusant

By using antifusant it is possible to paint on the surface of the silk as though it were paper. In this way, you can have greater control of the brushstrokes. This is because the pores of the fabric do not absorb the dye with the same degree of intensity when it has been treated with antifusant.

We will use the petrol-based antifusant here because it allows us to work with steam-fixed dyes.

Adjust the consistency of the antifusant: the dye will blot if the antifusant applied is too liquid.

The dye will form drops and dry irregularly if the antifusant is too thick.

This is how the colors should act together if the antifusant has the correct consistency.

Classic technique, watery, and *ikat* effects

Prior designs on plant-based paper are not prepared for the classic technique, since the interesting thing about this process, given that it enables us to paint on silk as though it were paper, is that we can create pieces of work that are more direct and so have a certain air of spontaneity about them. This is the printing technique that uses natural templates.

Nor do we make any prior designs for the watery effect technique, although we will have examples in mind reminiscent of the movement of water.

Ikat is an Asian fabric with a very particular design. Characteristic for this fabric is that its coloring does not have definite lines. This effect can be imitated perfectly on silk with a specific technique.

3 Step by step
CLASSIC TECHNIQUE

In this example we have chosen a few leaves with a very special texture so that we can experiment with their positioning on the fabric and the pattern that will still remain when the fabric is treated with antifusant.

1. Although we are not using a prior design, you can get ideas from other pieces of work with a naturalistic theme that have also been created by using antifusant.

2. Equipment and materials needed for applying this technique: steam-fixed dye, antifusant, Essence F, bottle of water, glass jar, sponge for applying backgrounds, templates — in this case, real leaves—brushes for painting on silk, flat, stiff paintbrush, rags, and a hairdrier.

3. After outlining the edges of the scarf with transparent gutta, pour a small quantity of antifusant into a jar.

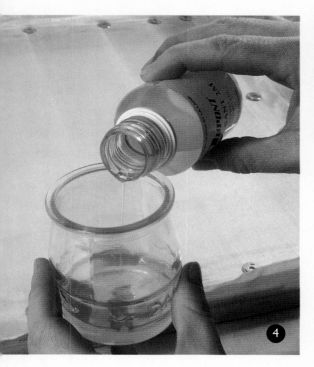

4. Now pour a few drops of Essence F into the jar containing the antifusant to reduce the thickness of the liquid.

5. To create the background, impregnate the sponge with the antifusant that has been diluted with Essence F and then squeeze it out. So that it does not drip too much, spread the antifusant with the sponge without overlapping any of the applications.

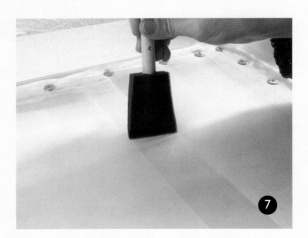

6. Begin by sliding the sponge vertically, starting from one of the edges of the frame.

7. Continue using the sponge to complete the whole of the background and then leave this to dry. The texture of the silk will soon lose its natural hang and the fabric will be rough, but quite ready for painting and for creating effects on the surface.

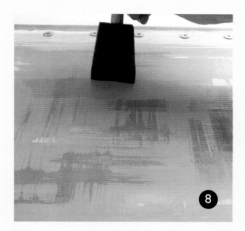

8. Once the antifusant you have spread over the surface of the silk is dry, you can begin to paint a background with the brown dye.

9. Now paint the roughest side of the leaves by using a colored dye that will stand out in the composition.

10. Once the background is dry, continue with the initial naturalistic theme and start to paint the plants and branches in the composition in various shades of green and dark brown.

11. Use the leaf to print onto the surface of the treated cloth. You can repeat the printing operation by superimposing the leaf on the previous print to create an overlaid effect.

12. Using a fine paintbrush for silk (a Petit-gris), you can outline the edges of the printed leaves to confer greater authenticity to the piece.

13. Here is a detail of the outline of the printed leaf.

14. The final appearance before fixing the silk;
the cloth will recover its natural texture only
after dry-cleaning.

4 Step by step
TECHNIQUE WITH WATERY EFFECT

Here we will use the same materials as for the classic technique, although we will apply other colors, in this case predominantly blues, as well as using cotton buds. However, with this technique we do not dilute the antifusant with Essence F because we want the surface of the silk to stay more compact; nevertheless, it will serve as an outliner.

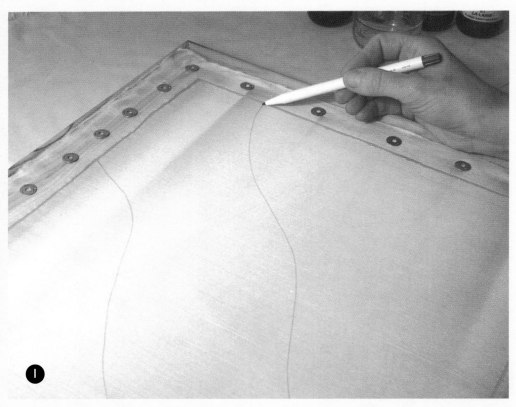

1. Once the edge of the silk has been marked with transparent gutta you can begin to trace undulating shapes with the Petit-gris paintbrush, simply by wetting it in water.

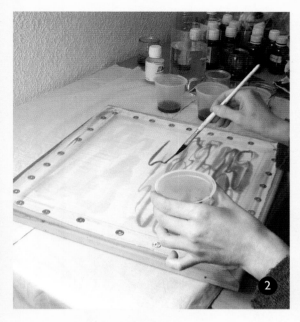

2. Apply a light blue dye just above the wavy lines that you have made with water.

3. Continue tracing over the lines of water with the blue dye, which, on mixing with the wet areas on the surface, will give a dégradé (graduated) effect.

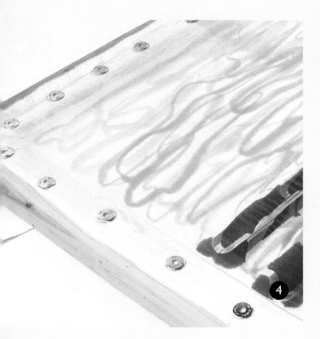

4. When the dye is dry, apply the antifusant, either with a cotton bud or a stiff brush, following the wavy lines of the water patterns previously created.

5. After the areas where the antifusant has been applied have dried, you can begin to create an intermittent background with a sponge coated with navy blue dye from a bottle. Start by painting the lower part of the fabric horizontally.

6. When you have finished the intermittent navy blue background you will see that the wavy lines where you applied the antifusant stand out with a more intense color. This contrast is more marked when the silk is still wet, since drying tends to unify the colors of all the water patterns.

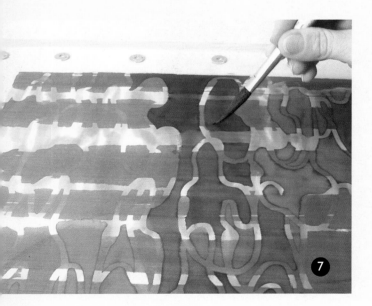

7. In order to break up this color uniformity and maintain the contrast between the dark and light blues on the wet silk, it is a good idea to repaint with navy blue over the zones where there were no lines of antifusant.

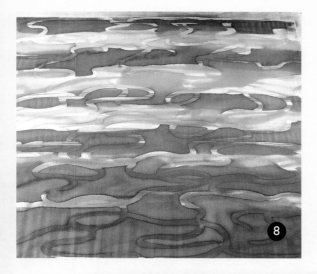

8. Through the interplay of the antifusant and the dyes applied in undulating shapes you will have achieved an effect imitating water's freedom of movement.

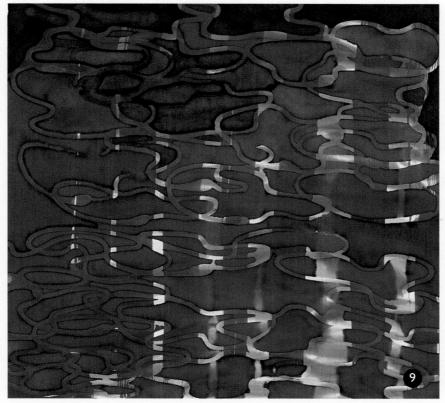

9. Detail of the finished work: note that the lightest areas are those where the greatest quantity of antifusant was applied.

5 Step by step
TECHNIQUE WITH IKAT EFFECT

With this technique, the printed effect that this material acquires is due to the dye spreading wherever the silk has not been treated with antifusant. The dye concentrates in the areas that are antifusant-treated.

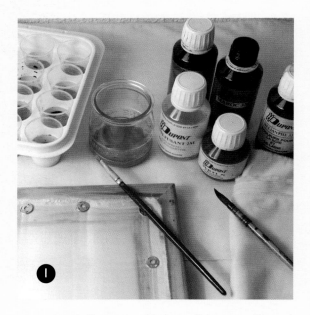

1. To create the ikat effect you will need: antifusant, gutta, stretching frame, pongé silk, flat, stiff paintbrush No. 0 for painting on silk, glass jar, brown, ultramarine blue, ivy green, and yellow dyes.

2. Once the stretching frame has been set up and the edges have been marked with transparent gutta, wet the stiff paintbrush with a solution prepared in the glass jar and composed of the antifusant plus a few drops of gutta, which provides a thicker liquid more suitable for painting on silk with a flat paintbrush. Paint the silk with this antifusant in vertical lines placed parallel to each other, with a small space left between each one so that they do not seem to overlap. Note that you do not have a complete layer of antifusant: this will be important when you want the silk to accept another color painted on top.

3. When you have applied the lines of antifusant and this has dried – a process that you can speed up with a hairdrier – you can begin to trace a design in various colors using the silk paintbrush. You will see that when a line is painted the silk responds by acquiring a very curious pattern: the dye does not appear in a linear form, but is blurred, creating the ikat effect.

4. Continue painting with the silk paintbrush along the whole surface, changing the colors and mixing them in different jars until an attractive design is achieved.

5. Here the final result is an imitation of Japanese ikat fabrics. The use of the antifusant causes hardening, so the feel of the silk becomes coarser. This effect on the fabric soon disappears with fixing and dry-cleaning.

The ikat technique offers many attractive possibilities.

Dégradé

The *dégradé* or graduated background consists of a zone of differing degrees of the same color which go from light to dark or from dark to light. We can also achieve this effect with contrasting colors by following the same procedure.

In order to paint a *dégradé* we have to be sure that the silk is very taut on the frame because otherwise the wet material could be ruined, especially if it is crepe de chine. Obviously, so that the liquid dye does not seep outside the stretched silk we also have to trace a line of gutta around the inside edge of the frame.

This is a rapid technique since variegation of color is achieved when the applied dye is wet; therefore it is a good idea to paint quickly, so that it does not dry out. Precisely because of this immediacy it is very important to prepare the quantities of dye necessary to paint the whole background and to organize the paintbrushes, sponges, and other materials before beginning work.

6 Step by step

MULTICOLORED DÉGRADÉ

This technique was created by Nadia Faus, who is an established expert in print design and painting on silk techniques.

In order to obtain multicolored *dégradé*, Nadia has chosen contrasting dyes of varying shades, such as ultramarine blue, light blue, light green, and yellow. The distribution of the colors in the jars has been organized going from dark to light. In addition to the dyes, we will need: a bottle of water, one or two silk paintbrushes, a rag to dry them with, and sponges.

1. First, mix concentrated solvent with distilled water in the proportion of 1½ fl oz (40 ml) solvent per 1¾ pints (1 liter) of water. This allows you to spread the dye more easily in order to obtain a more authentic *dégradé*.

2. When pouring the dye into a jar, add a few drops of the concentrated solvent and distilled water solution.

3. With the solvent mixture combined in the dyes, the result is certain to be brilliant and intense.

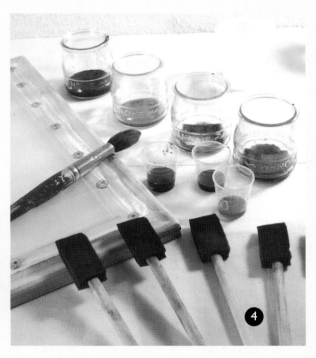

4. The equipment and materials used to paint *dégradé*.

5. Arrange the jars with the quantities of dye that you will need to achieve a multicolored *dégradé* effect.

6. Start by making a short line of dark dye in one of the corners of the silk.

8. Immediately mix violet tones together with the black in this background.

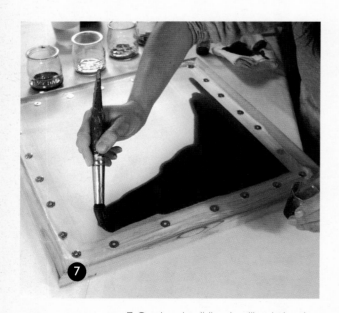

7. Continue by sliding the silk paintbrush rapidly across the material.

9. Continue varying the violet and dark shades while always aiming to spread the dye in a single direction.

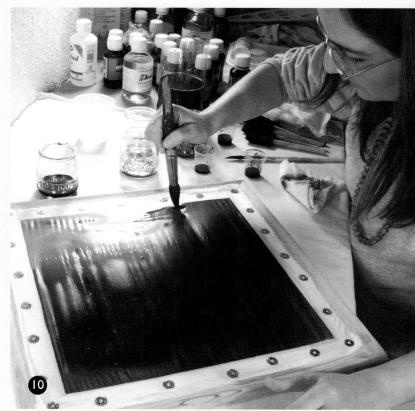

10. Add the oranges and reddish shades while not interrupting the variegated effect of the color emerging from the violet and leave a small space white to paint with a light tone that will stand out in the composition.

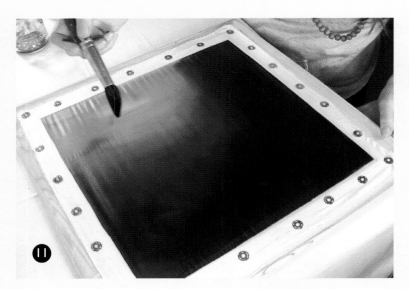

11. The yellow gives the final touch to the piece of work as it stands out spectacularly against a background of violets and dark shades.

12. Once the dyes are dry, the intensity of the color is less pronounced, but with the subsequent fixing and washing of the silk it will soon be recovered.

Multicolored *dégradé* with toned-down dyes

Another possibility with the concentrated solvent and distilled water solution is to lower the tone of the color of the dyes. Here, Nadia carries out another exercise, similar to the previous one, but with other dyes toned down with solution.

Multicolored dégradé: the final result.

Begin with a brushstroke of ultramarine blue and tone it down to a light blue and then to a green. From the light green the yellow is reached, which provides the final interesting touch.

Hint

Immediately after each color application, go back to the line where the dyes overlap and mix them by dragging your half-dry brush forwards from the back. Never add any more dye or try to change the color once the dye has begun to dry. This could produce marks and stripes.

In this example, the artist has chosen a blue and a red dye and has arranged the pots according to the percentages of dye needed to create the design. So, from left to right, the pots contain: 100% pure blue dye, 75% blue and 25% red dye, 75% red and 25% blue dye, and 100% pure red dye.

Two-color *dégradé*

To obtain two-color *dégradé* it is recommended that you choose two pure colors that are quite contrasting and place the percentage of the dyes required in the jars in order to be ready to paint. The necessary equipment and materials needed, as with the multicolor *dégradé*, are: one or two silk paintbrushes, a jar of water (used to soften the color), and a rag to dry it.

To start with, it is best to prepare and organize a succession of three to five shades of a specific color. Then you can apply the lightest shade of color first and continue adding the others successively, going from one side of the material to the other, until you end up with the darkest shade last of all.

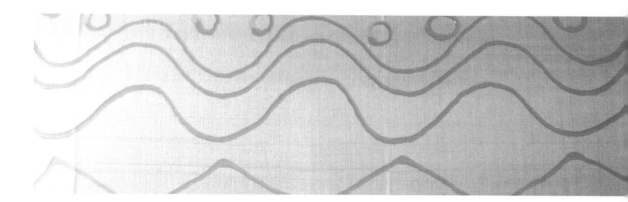

Painting with thickeners

If you wish to work more freely, using an outliner but without making lines with gutta, the vegetable gum solution that makes up thickener allows you to produce more creative and spontaneous works of art.

Thickener has a gelatinous consistency and can be mixed with the dyes, resulting in a paste that lets you paint on silk as though you were working with oil paint. Make sure that the mixture is the right consistency because, if it is too liquid, it will fade and smudge the lines. The best proportion to use is 50% dye and 50% thickener, which results in a quite dense solution that can be spread with a flat paintbrush or a spatula.

Like gutta, thickener acts as an outliner, but is much more fragile, though, like gutta, it creates a cardboard-like texture that disappears with fixing and washing.

Thickener is slow to dry but it can be applied even when wet because then it makes a stronger barrier than when it is dry.

Normally, using thickener does not allow us to complete very detailed designs because it is difficult to make fine brushstrokes with this substance.

Finally, do not forget that all the materials that we use with thickener can be cleaned afterwards with water.

7

Step by step
TRANSPARENT THICKENER

In this technique, the purpose of the thickener is very simple: we use it as an outliner so that we can spread different dyes over the silk. This time, the design will be colored with unmodified dyes to produce an attractive result and to demonstrate that, even without any lightening of the tones, simple and pretty artworks can easily be created.

1. Here is the design that we will create on silk. The drawing is very simple since the technique of using a thickener does not allow for very detailed work.

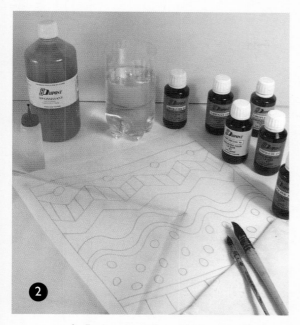

2. Equipment and materials we will use to apply this technique: plant-based paper, stretching frame, thickener, check paintbrush for silk, stiff paintbrush for spreading the thickener, and colored dyes (magenta, cyan blue, orange, and violet).

3. The transparent thickener and plastic applicator with wide nozzle for applying the lines of thick outliner.

4. Carefully fill the applicator with thickener.

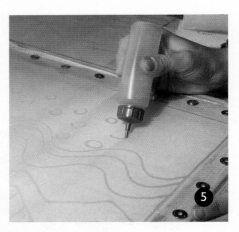

5. First mark a margin round the silk with gutta. Then, with the drawing of the design under the stretching frame, trace the lines with thickener using the applicator, as though they were lines of gutta.

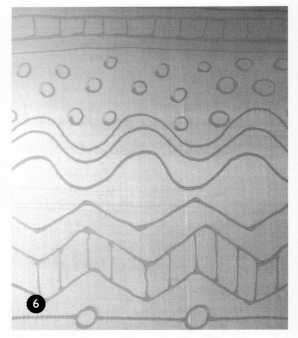

6. The lines of thickener have now been applied as a resist, outlining the areas that are going to be painted.

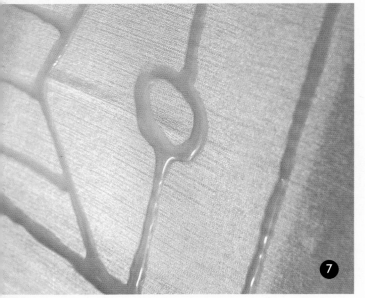

7. Detail of the lines drawn with the thickener. They act as an outliner but are weaker than gutta. Remember that the thickener is slow to dry and when it is wet it makes a far better resistant.

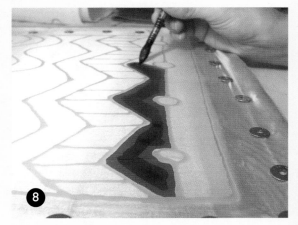

8. Begin by painting the lower part of the design with a brown dye and then add different colors, however you wish, over the whole surface of the silk.

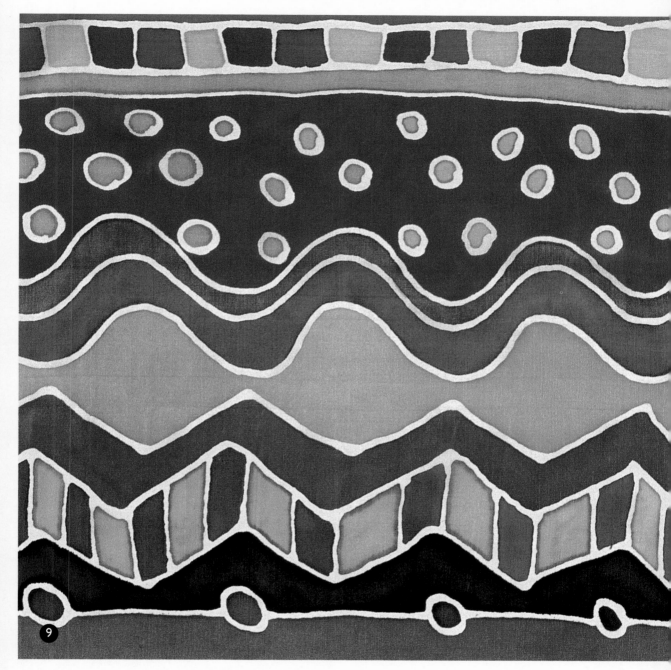

9. Here is the finished result of this project, created using transparent thickener, with a combination of contrasting colors.

8 Step by step
COLORED THICKENER

There are other ways of using thickener, as this exercise will show. This time it fulfills the function of a dye although, because of its density, you cannot spread the thickener over the silk in a uniform way like paint. It does, however, allow you to draw freely because the silk reacts with the thickener as though it were paper, so the color does not disperse and you are able to have control over the design.

1. For this technique we use practically the same materials as with the transparent thickener, except that, instead of applying different colors, this time we are producing an interesting piece of work with only two colors: a brown and an olive green.

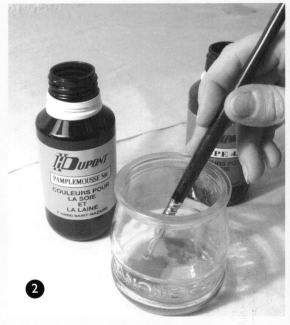

2. First of all, obtain the olive green by mixing a brown with a basic green. Remember that when you apply the thickener to the dye mix the color will tend to lighten in tone.

3. Now add the thickener to the olive green mix until the combination becomes as thick as honey. You will have a thickener solution that is tinted with color.

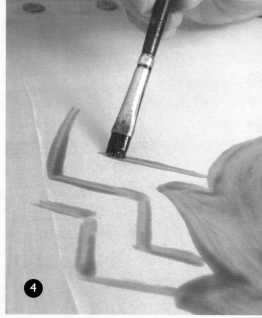

4. Once you have some idea of what you want to draw, but without any prior design on plant-based paper, start to carefully trace out the motif with the colored thickener solution using a flat, stiff paintbrush.

5. When you have finished painting the motif with thickener, and without waiting for it to dry (so it can function better as an outliner), start to paint over the design using the second dye. This color can be used directly from the pot of dye, without being mixed with any external substance.

6. When you are painting the silk with the brown dye, you will soon see how the design made with the colored thickener acts as an outliner.

7. Here is the finished result, achieved using the colored thickener technique.

Step by step
FALSE BATIK

By making an impression with wet esparto grass on top of the thickener you can imitate the typical crackle or breaking up effect of batik. The result is called false batik, and it produces a convincing effect on silk.

2. To create a false batik you will need: dyes, thickener, silk paintbrushes, one small and one large stiff paintbrush, water, glass jars, dish, esparto grass, and an invisible ink pen.

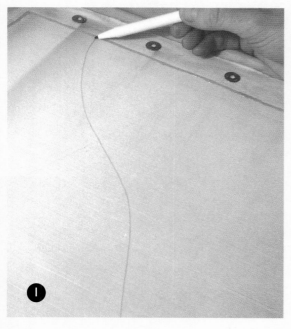

1. With an invisible ink pen, start by drawing the lines that will act as your guide for painting the scarf. The idea is for them to appear to be painted flowing diagonally.

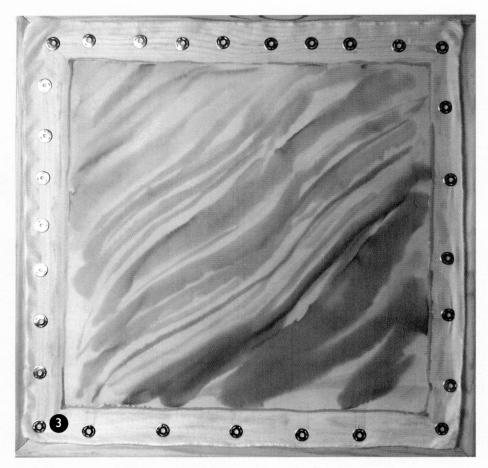

3. Finish off the diagonal brushstrokes over the whole scarf with some lighter and some darker lines, applying water with one medium brush and one wide one, so that the background does not appear uniform. This is necessary for the steps that follow.

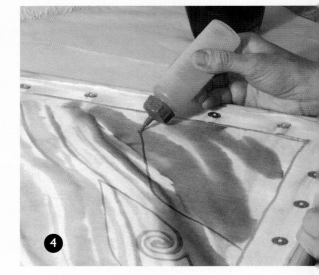

4. Once the dyes have dried, begin to draw new lines with the thickener that will act as outlines for other images.

5. Finish drawing the lines of thickener acting as outliners on the silk.

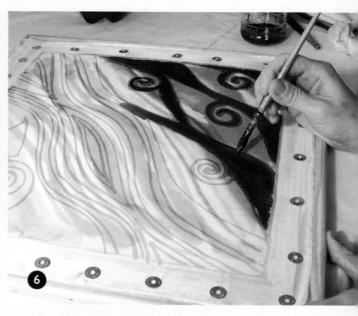

6. Now start painting in turquoise blue on the lower right-hand section.

7. Finish the layer of blue over the whole surface, leaving the insides of the outlined motifs free and letting the diagonal brush-strokes show through.

8. While you wait for the dye and thickener to dry in the dish, prepare another solution of thickener mixed with brown dye.

9. When the thickener and the dye are dry, wet the esparto grass in the prepared brown thickener solution.

10. Once the esparto grass has been dampened, wipe it on a rag or a piece of adhesive tape so that when you wipe it over the painted silk scarf, it does not deposit too much thickener. Continue wiping the esparto over the entire painted surface to imitate the crackle of the batik technique.

11. This is the finished result, with its marine atmosphere, of using the false batik technique on silk.

10 Step by step
PICTORIAL EFFECTS

It is very easy to achieve pictorial effects on silk using thickener. You need to know how to apply the thickener and to paint with contrasting tones in strategic areas in order to obtain the desired result.

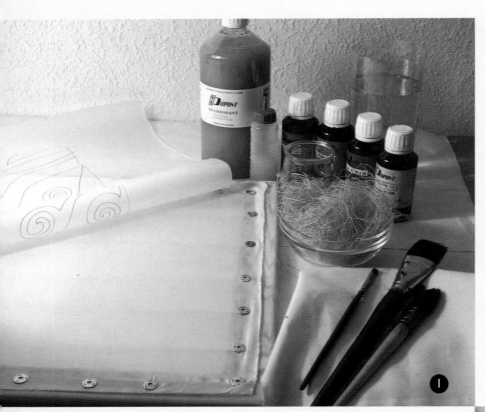

1. To create pictorial effects with thickener you need, in addition to the usual materials from the previous techniques: a spatula or a stiff, wide paintbrush.

2. In a pot, mix some thickener with a violet dye in the proportion three parts thickener to one of dye.

3. Pour the transparent thickener over the silk.

4. Spread the transparent and the colored thickeners out with the spatula or the flat, wide brush, leaving blank spaces for adding other colors to further enliven this pictorial composition.

5. Using the blocking outlines you can fill in the blank spaces with a dye that contrasts with the background.

6. Sometimes so-called "swimming pools" are produced (an excess of liquid on the surface of the silk).

7. By applying different colors in this composition you can obtain a pictorial effect. As the thickener has been poured on, the texture of the silk will be very rough, but once it has been fixed and washed with water the viscosity of the outlining glue will disappear and the fabric will return to its natural state.

Step by step
IMPRESSIONISTIC EFFECTS

Another characteristic of thickener is its ability to achieve impressionistic effects. By mixing it with dyes and superimposing it onto other tones, you can make the coloring of the natural background stand out and, at the same time, add a special spontaneity.

2. Start by applying the mixture to the silk using the same stiff paintbrush with which you prepared the dye earlier.

1. Using the same materials as with the previous technique, make a mixture of thickener and green dye. In this example, we are creating a naturalistic design, with as much spontaneity as possible.

4. Leave one corner and several other spaces, such as the flower, blank so you can apply other dyes. Here the green thickener acts as an outliner in the design.

3. Continue stretching out the green thickener from the outlines to achieve a textured effect for the background.

5. Paint the blank spaces in different colored dyes to give the picture varied tones.

6. You can mix colors and, by adding water, soften the tones of them.

7. You can superimpose more green thickener onto the applied colors to create still more effects in this impressionist image of nature.

 3.2. Complementary techniques

Once you have consolidated the basic skills of painting on silk you can begin to try out new methods involving the application of salt crystals and alcohol. The techniques in this chapter are called complementary because they can be combined with others to create textured backgrounds over which you can work using gutta and other silk painting materials.

Salt techniques

The principle underpinning this technique is that salt attracts and absorbs moisture. When salt crystals are spread over a surface of painted silk, they respond by absorbing the wet dye, creating highly evocative shapes. Through familiarizing yourself with the dyes and how they react with salt, you will learn how to use the technique and so come to master it for creating motifs or pictorial backgrounds according to your taste.

By using various sizes of salt crystal you can obtain different effects because they do not all attract the dye in the same way. For a good result, it is best to use sea salt, table salt, or mineral salt, but never the salt that is used for dishwashers.

Bear in mind that salt crystals work better on medium or strong colors than on pastel tones, since these are too soft to form vigorous textures.

The variety of textures which salt produces when applied over painting on silk depends on different factors: the number and size of the salt crystals, their location on the silk, and when they are added to the painted surface (since there will be a different result depending on whether this is before or after the dye). Equally influential are the weight and dampness of the silk, its response to the drying process, as well as the temperature, the humidity, and the air currents that may be present in the area where you are working.

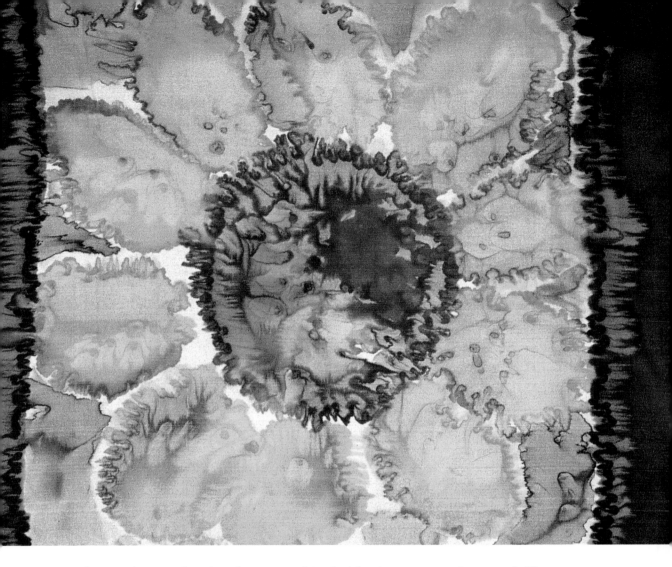

If you wish to use the salt technique combined with other processes, for example if you want to trace gutta on top, first allow the dye to dry completely. Afterwards carefully remove the salt crystals: make sure there are none left, since any remaining on the surface could give you a disagreeable surprise at a later stage. In fact, salt residue could make part of the texture of the silk rough and interfere with the application of the lines of gutta. In order to be certain about the sealing, make the lines of gutta a little thicker than usual.

Hint

Be careful with the paintbrushes that are used for this technique as they will pick up part of the excess salt and contaminate the dyes you are using. Contaminated dye will not spread uniformly, so it is advisable to label and keep apart the brushes and the excess dye to use on projects that do not require uniformity or neatness. Never mix contaminated dye with clean colors.

12 Step by step
GUIDED SALT EFFECTS

In this project we will carry out the first exercise in using salt crystals by guiding the salt, in this case imitating a very simple flower, to which lively colors will be added. We will experiment with the different ways in which the colors evolve due to the effect of the grains of sea salt on the silk.

1. Distribute the salt crystals with the aid of a spatula in the shape of a simple flower.

2. The equipment and materials needed for this technique are: water, spatula, rag, paintbrushes, yellow, brown, green, and orange dyes, sea salt, and silk paintbrushes.

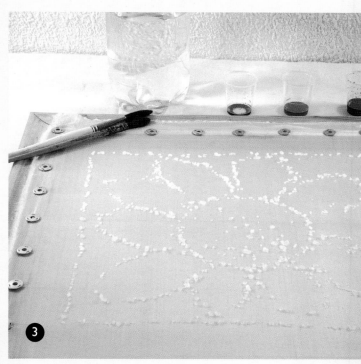

3. To the very simple drawing made with the salt you can now apply the dyes that you have already prepared in the pots as in the previous techniques. The salt will act as a barrier for the dyes, creating some very special effects.

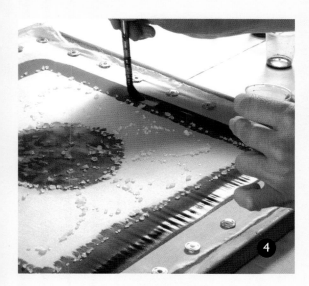

4. Begin by painting the edge of the flower from the other side, first with a turquoise blue and then with a dark green. Also, make some brushstrokes in the center of the flower with different colors, which will begin to react with the salt crystals that have been added.

6. After a short time you can see that the salt crystals will begin to absorb the dye and produce the first effects on the silk.

5. Paint the petals with yellow and orange, and reinforce the edge with a dark green so that the shape of them stands out.

7. You can then apply more dye to change the overall effect as you require.

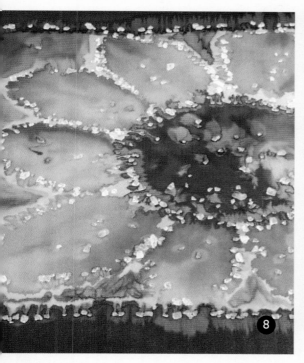

8. Leave the salt crystals to work their magic and wait for the dye spread over the silk to dry.

9. Add more salt crystals in any areas you choose in order to create a range of effects on the applied dyes.

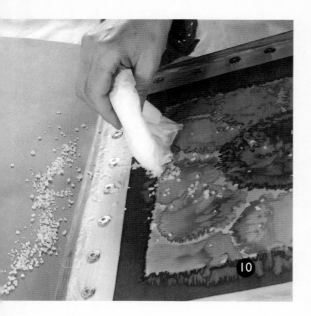

10. Remove the salt only when the dyes are dry. The crystals need to be gently removed with a rag or a piece of paper, being careful that none remain on the silk or on the work table because they could contaminate any equipment you may need to work with later on.

11. Here is the finished result of the project
using the guided salt technique.

12. This is another example of a design made
with guided salt.

13 Step by step
SCATTERED SALT EFFECTS

Another way of achieving pictorial effects with salt crystals involves scattering them randomly over the colors covering the silk. Because they are not deliberately placed so that they form a specific design, the result cannot be anticipated but is nonetheless equally attractive.

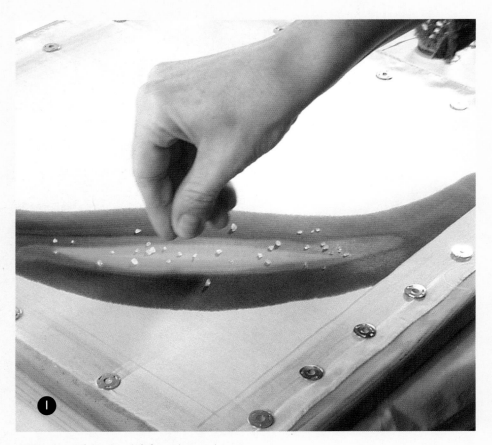

1. Make use of the dyes left from the previous project, since they are already contaminated with the salt crystals, and paint on the silk with a range of different green and yellow shades. Scatter the salt crystals while you paint, making sure the dye is wet enough for the salt to work. If you wait until the dye is dry, the salt will not have any effect.

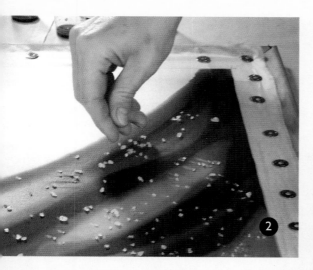

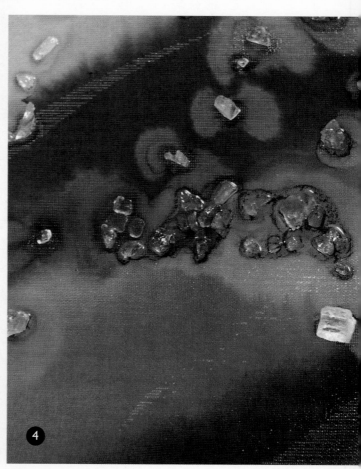

2. While you are waiting for the salt crystals to work, continue painting other color ranges and adding more sea salt crystals. Bear in mind that if you put down too much salt, the silk might fail to react and so produce less spectacular effects.

3. A picture of the salt while it is working. This is the time when it is allowed to settle before completely drying out. It is scattered over the silk that has been painted spontaneously with different brushstrokes of contrasting colors.

4. Detail of the process: you can see how the salt crystals react on the silk by absorbing the dye and leaving small halos of a lighter shade than the underlying color.

5. Here is the finished result of the project using the scattered salt technique. This scarf is already fixed and washed.

Hint

When you work with the salt technique it is advisable for the silk to be made quite wet with the dyes; if the silk is only slightly damp, the salt will not work.

Techniques using alcohol

When a drop of isopropyl alcohol is allowed to fall onto the surface of painted silk, it continues to spread until it forms a stain. The alcohol tends to push the pigment towards the area outside the stain, creating a ring of color that is darker than its surroundings. Once it is dry, this stain will have a slightly lighter color in the center, while the ring that surrounds it is darker.

You can use alcohol, therefore, to push dye from one location to another and, if you do this systematically with some design in mind, you can develop magnificent effects and textures. When you start to experiment with this particular technique it is best to do so on dry backgrounds to which a medium or thick layer of dye has previously been applied.

The shape and size of the stain depend on the size of the paintbrush and the amount of alcohol. If the dye is completely dry before applying the alcohol, the displacement of color effect increases.

On the other hand, excellent pictorial effects can also be achieved by brushing on alcohol and applying color to dry silk.

14
Step by step
MOTHER-OF-PEARL AND MARBLE EFFECTS

Part one

1. Before beginning to paint, draw the shape of an imaginary shell above some sea waves on a piece of plant-based paper.

3. For this technique you need: transparent petrol-based gutta, an applicator, alcohol, crimson, ultramarine blue, and brown colored dyes, jar for pouring the alcohol, water, paint-brushes for silk, rag, and a small hairdrier.

2. Once the margin has been marked with transparent gutta and drops of Essence F have been added to reduce the density of the gutta in the applicator, start to trace the lines of gutta following the previously drawn design. This time choose a very fine nib for the applicator, so be careful not to perforate the silk when applying the gutta.

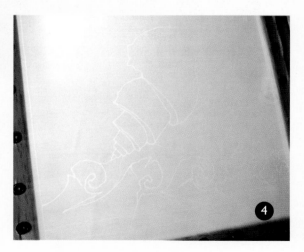

4. Once again, make sure that the gutta is properly sealed. To ensure the seal is good, you can dry the gutta with a small hairdrier so that it penetrates the silk appropriately.

5. Pour the alcohol into the jar to use later on and once the gutta is dry, you can begin to paint the mother-of-pearl effects on the shell.

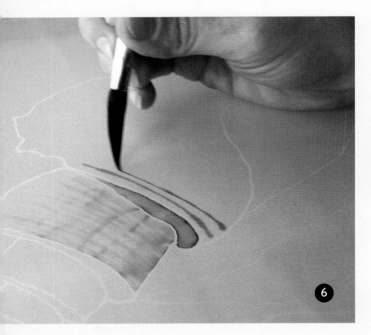

6. Paint the mother-of-pearl effects by applying fine brushstrokes of a very dark color, which in this example is a sepia brown. First, draw lines in one direction, then very rapidly brush on water in the opposite direction to the already painted lines, so that the color breaks up and creates interesting effects.

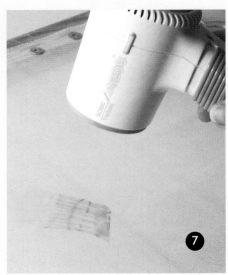

7. Dry the resulting effects when you are happy with them otherwise the water will continue to react and can completely blur them, leaving just a few dark marks behind.

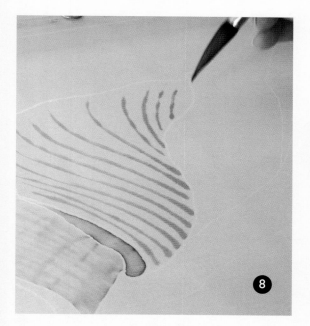

8. Continue working the mother-of-pearl effect over the entire shell with your brush.

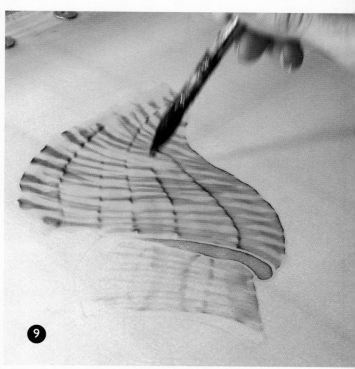

9. Add an ultramarine blue to improve the mother-of-pearl quality and continue with the same procedure of laying down the color in one direction and then, very quickly, brushing on water in the opposite direction. So the color, which in this case comprises the two shades of brown and blue, breaks down to form interesting transparent effects.

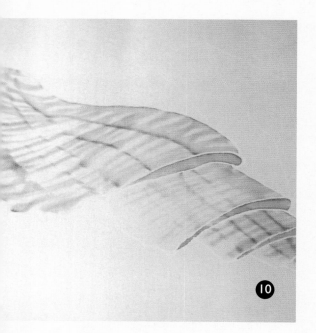

10. Here is the final mother-of-pearl effect applied to the shell.

11. Continue painting the broken-up design drawn with gutta in the lower right-hand area with the brown and blue tones diluted with water in certain areas. In this way you can create the marble effect.

12. A detail of the marble effect that can be achieved with color.

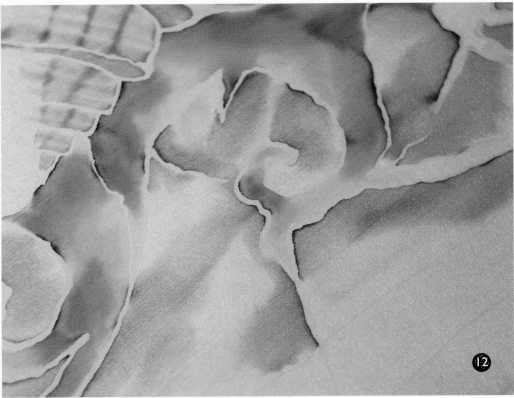

13. Continue adding alcohol to the painted areas with a paintbrush. The alcohol creates cracks on the small painted surfaces because it displaces the pigment.

14. One way of stopping the break-up of pigment caused by the alcohol is to dry the affected area immediately whenever you like the effect that this has created. Continue to apply the hairdrier in all the small areas, and you can even add more dye if necessary to create more contrasting effects.

15. If you practice with the hairdrier and then use it at the same time as applying the alcohol with the paintbrush, you can displace the pigment that has been affected by the alcohol in several directions: with practice you can make it go in the direction you want. In this way you can create a marble effect or the evocative impression produced by a whole network of small cracks.

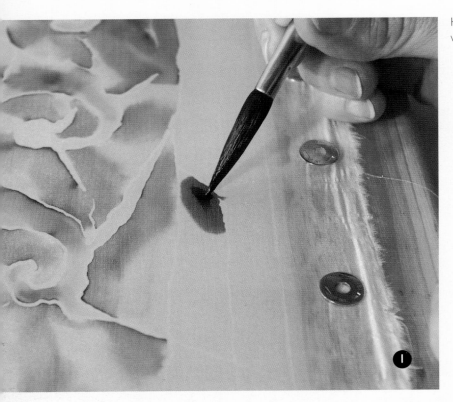

How to correct a mistake
when sealing with gutta

1. Start by painting green at the picture's edge,
which is broken up like a mosaic by gutta.

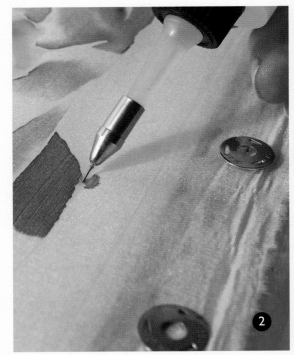

2. This area has not been correctly sealed so
the dye runs over the edge of the small space
that has been outlined by the gutta. To prevent
the dye from leaking, you need to apply gutta
rapidly to the edge of the picture where the
color has escaped.

3. In the same area, combat the flow of the dye by applying a circle of alcohol around the stain with a cotton bud.

4. Note how the dye mark quickly disappears as you rub the affected area with the alcohol-soaked cotton bud.

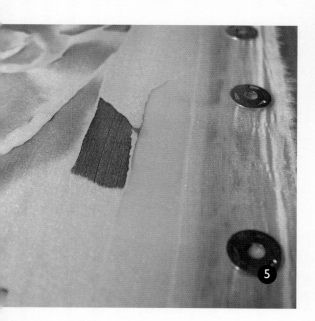

5. You can repeat the same operation several times, applying alcohol to the area and absorbing it with the cotton bud until the dye is well diluted. The dye stain never completely disappears, however.

15

Step by step
PART TWO

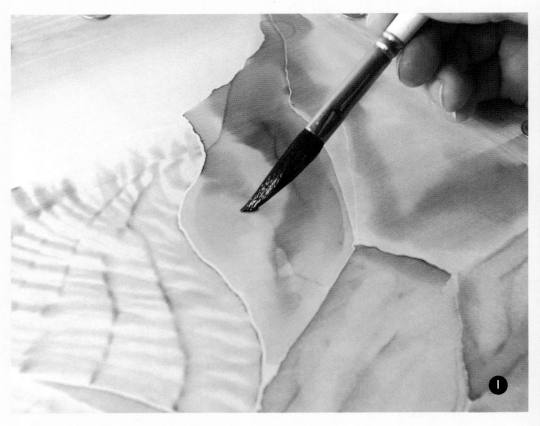

1. An effect of aging can be obtained on silk by wetting the paintbrush in alcohol and adding a little yellow dye.

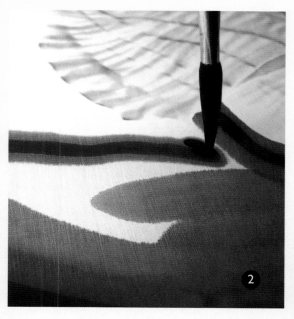

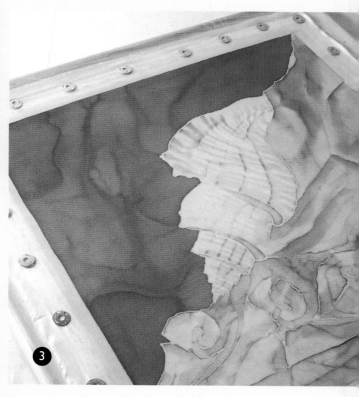

2. Begin painting the upper right-hand area of the shell in crimson to give a more contrasting effect. Spread all the dye with large and firm brushstrokes to create grooves.

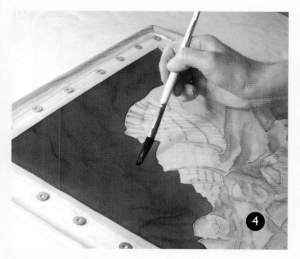

3. Add some brushstrokes of alcohol to the crimson surface, causing displacement of the pigment that breaks up the surface.

4. If the result is not sufficiently contrasting as here, you can repeat the operation with strokes from the brush soaked in alcohol. In this way continue to create more grooves and give greater depth to the surface.

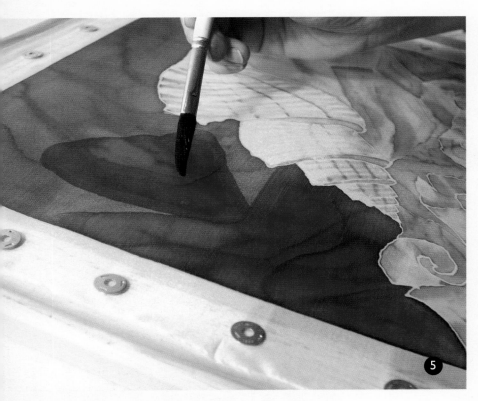

5. A detail of the application of alcohol on the crimson background, where you can see more clearly the effects of the grooves that it leaves behind.

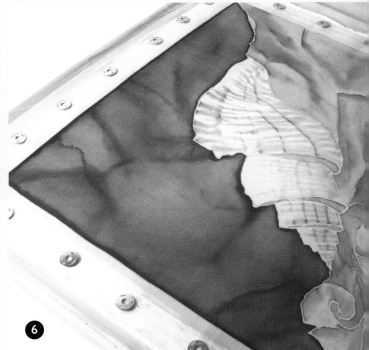

6. In fact, you can continue adding layers of alcohol until you achieve the desired effect. In this case you wish to create depth.

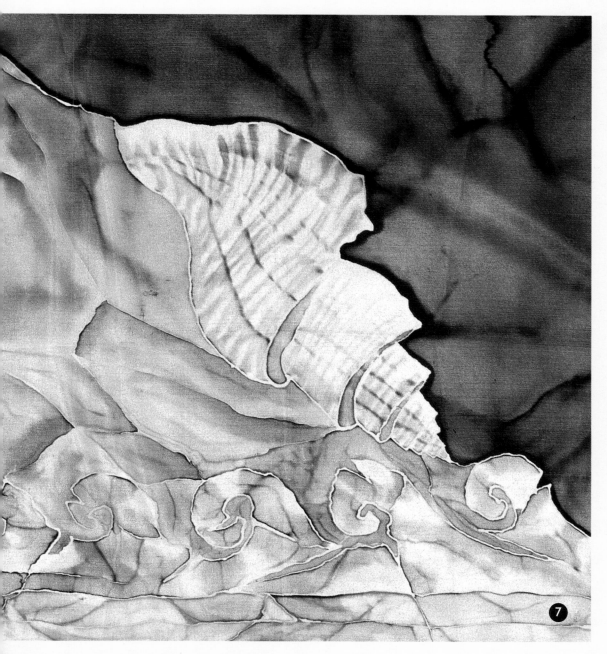

7. This is the interesting final result following the laborious task of using alcohol to create mother-of-pearl and marble effects.

16 Step by step
DRIP AND DISTRESSED MARBLE EFFECTS

Part one

You can reuse the alcohol dilutant, but this time with a dropper, to achieve the watery effects of a marine theme. In addition to creating an aquatic texture, you can add a motif that is both in keeping with the water theme and also reminiscent of distressed marble, for which the main process includes using antifusant spread on the silk with a natural sponge.

The drying process and the subsequent application of alcohol displaces the pigment which, with a little practice, you can direct to wherever you want in order to create a more sculptural effect, though you can never make it disappear.

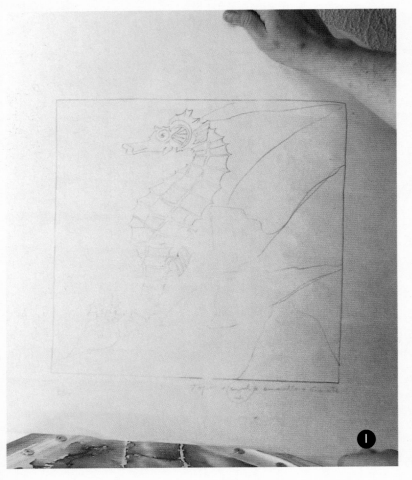

1. Dripping is an ideal technique for creating bubbly atmospheres. In this case you are creating a marine theme consisting of two parts: on the left you will use the drip method and on the right you will produce the distressed marble effects. The two spaces are separated by a sea horse motif.

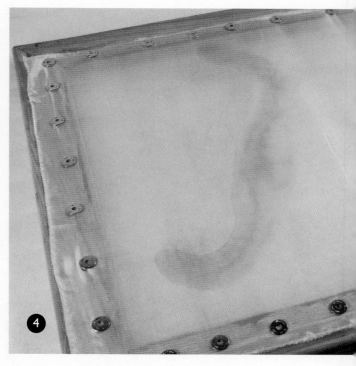

2. For this new technique (really two different ways of working – the drip effect and the distressed marble effect) you need, as well as the silk, a frame, alcohol, antifusant, transparent gutta, dropper, natural sponge, dish, paint-brushes for silk, a small wooden stick or cotton bud, and water.

4. Once the brushstroke of dye spread on the back of the sea horse has dried, mark the outline of its back with transparent gutta and continue up to the edge of the silk. The gutta will act as a barrier to the dyes that you will apply on both sides of the composition.

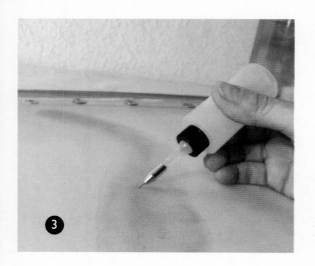

3. Remember to trace the gutta round the edge of the silk. For tracing the design use transparent gutta, not colored. A good way to prevent the white line from standing out excessively in the design is to paint the back of the sea horse with a very light dye.

6. Check that the sponge is sufficiently wrung out to spread the antifusant irregularly over the right-hand part of the composition.

5. Pour antifusant into the dish and with it wet the part of a natural sponge that has the most suitable sculptural texture. This will allow you to obtain the distressed marble effect later on.

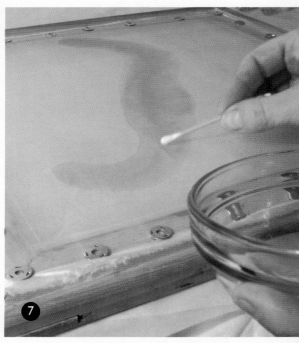

7. Wet the cotton bud or small wooden stick in the dish of antifusant and draw lines with it on the silk, imitating the broken-up pattern of marble. The antifusant acts as a barrier round each small surface outlined, so you can paint different dyes in each one.

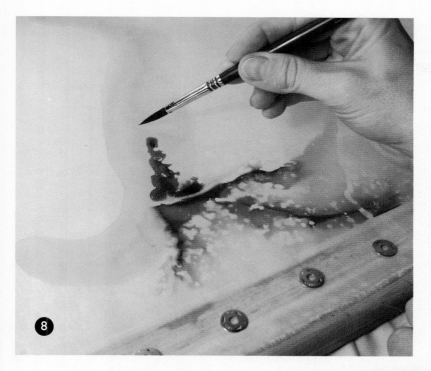

8. Once the antifusant has dried, which it does quickly, you can begin to paint each outlined area of the picture.

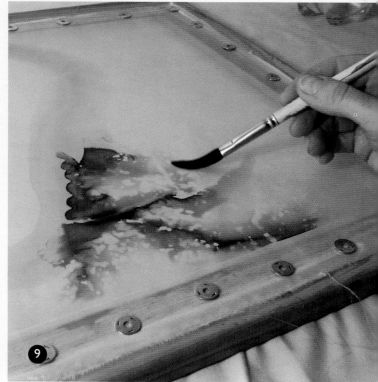

9. Continue by adding a dark dye and water, and note that the dabs of antifusant that you have applied with the sponge are beginning to have an effect because, when the water and dye are added, a texture appears in the form of patterns that are reminiscent of distressed marble.

10. These patterns will continue to appear while you are painting and, if you like the effect, you can apply the hairdrier to halt it. If you do not dry the silk, the breaking-up effect of imitation marble will reach the point where it fades away.

Step by step
PART TWO

1. Once the marble area has been completed you can start to paint the other side of the sea horse. Do this by making a *dégradé* with blue and brown dyes.

3. While you are waiting for the *dégradé* dyes to dry, you can see that the composition's two sections are completely set apart by the lighter colored central motif.

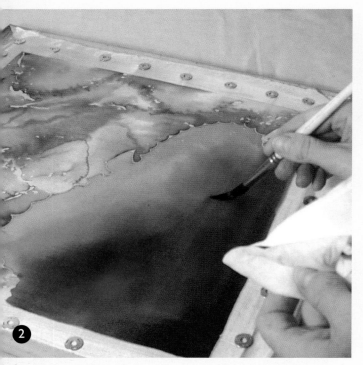

2. Continue developing the dark and light *dégradé*, starting with the sea horse, because you want this to stand out from the background that you are going to work on with the alcohol drip technique.

4. Trace the outline of the sea horse with a transparent gutta applicator, just as with the texture of the interior. Proceed carefully in order to follow the lines on the plant-based paper placed under the frame.

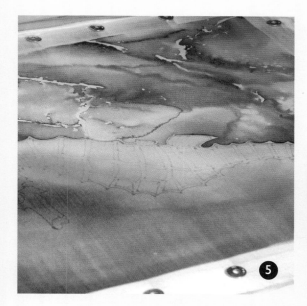

5. When the lines of gutta have been traced, wait for them to dry before using the alcohol drip technique.

6. Start to work with this new technique, using a dropper or a pipette, so alcohol once again determines the design.

7. Continue dripping alcohol over the *dégradé* surface and you will see the pigment being displaced outwards, creating a ring of color that is a little darker around the edge.

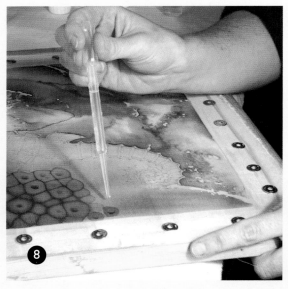

8. The resulting texture is an underwater design with bubbles produced by the drip technique, their size varying according to the amount of alcohol released by the dropper.

9. Repeat the drip technique but this time with a paintbrush dipped in alcohol in order to apply the texture to the inside of the sea horse. See how the alcohol displaces the pigment and creates volume by making the figure stand out.

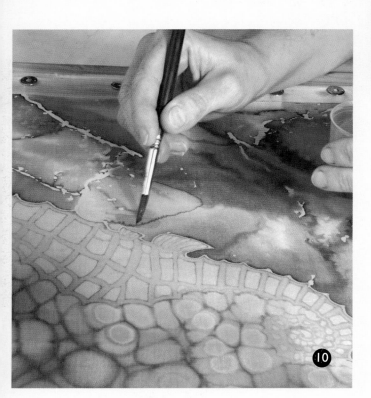

10. Using the same paintbrush dampened with alcohol, try to improve the effects in some of the distressed marble areas. You can do this by using the hairdrier to obtain the broken-up marble effect, as in the previous step by step.

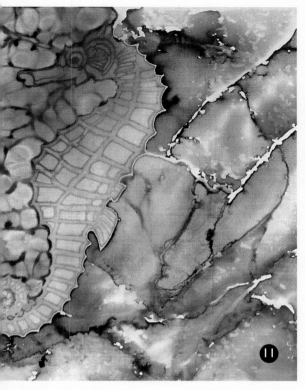

11. The finished image is very evocative of an underwater atmosphere and has an attractive central motif.

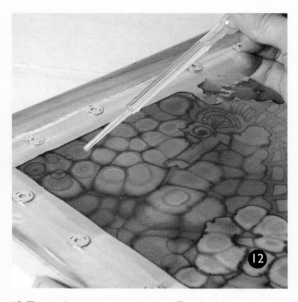

12. To obtain a more contrasting effect in the area where the drip technique was used, you can continue to apply the alcohol with the dropper. This repetition is called double dripping: its greater density of drops produces a more bubbly effect.

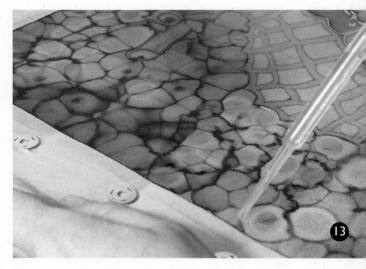

13. With double dripping you can continue creating a double texture, with a large number of circles around each drop of alcohol applied. The result is more contrasting than the previous effect.

Hint

When you apply dripped alcohol to a small part of a large, gutta-sealed surface, you must continue without pausing until you have completed the area, otherwise mountain-like shapes will appear, similar to those made by the dye of in an incorrectly made *dégradé*.

Results of the exercises using basic techniques after fixing and ironing the silk.

Result of the exercise using transparent gutta.

Colored gutta example: superimposition of gutta to create transparency.

Exercise using the classic technique.

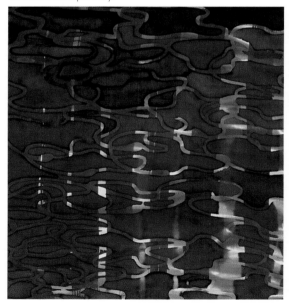

Result of the exercise to produce a watery effect.

Results of the exercises using basic techniques after fixing and ironing the silk.

Result of the ikat effect technique.

Example of multicolored *dégradé*.

Example of two-colored *dégradé*.

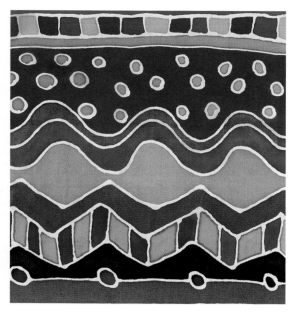

Result of the exercise using transparent thickener.

Results of the exercises using basic techniques after fixing and ironing the silk.

Result of applying the technique using colored thickener.

Example of the false batik technique.

Result of using thickener to create pictorial effects.

Example of painting with thickeners to create impressionistic effects.

Results of exercises using complementary techniques after fixing and ironing the silk.

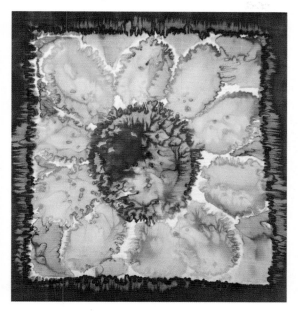

Result of the exercise using the guided salt technique.

Example of the scattered salt technique.

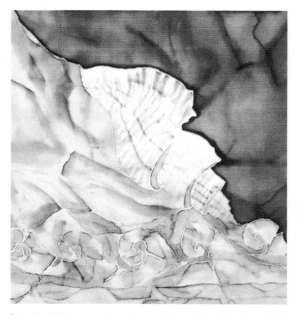

Result of the exercise using mother-of-pearl and marble effects.

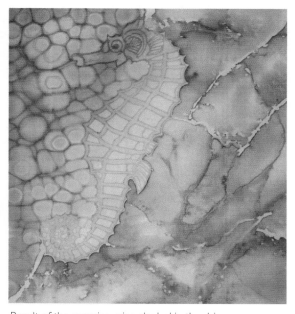

Result of the exercise using alcohol in the drip and distressed marble technique.

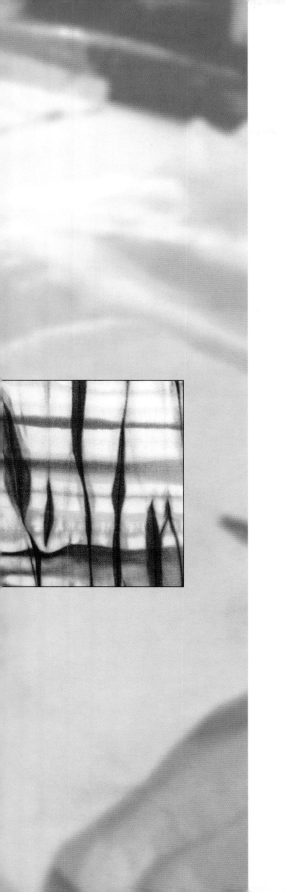

4

Dyeing, batik and fixing

4.1.Dyeing

Decorative dyeing of materials is a craft activity that usually affords a great deal of satisfaction. There are some simple methods with which you can achieve rapid results, and others that require more time and skill.

In ethnographic museums there are examples of African, Japanese, and Indian art which can help inspire you with new ideas. The dyeing technique is an ancient one, dating back to prehistoric times, yet even now it is considered to be a totally new art.

The central skill of the art of dyeing lies in knowing how to make decorative use of the areas that are set aside and those that are treated with a resist.

If different parts of a piece of material are tied, knotted, bound together, pleated or sewn, areas are formed that cannot be penetrated by the dye, or that will only allow a small amount through.

Equipment and materials

The basic equipment and materials you need are: fabric, dyes, salt, thread, containers for the dyes, and a work area large enough to wash out and dry the dyed fabrics.

The containers must be big enough to hold the fabrics comfortably, but not too big, so as not to waste the dye.

For washing out, a basin with running water is ideal, but a bucket or large bowl can also be used, as long as it is possible to change the water whenever necessary.

In addition to this equipment, you will need: small wooden or glass sticks for mixing the dye, rubber gloves, newspaper so as not to stain the working area, and screw-top jars or bottles in which to keep the dye.

Types of dye

Dyes can be classified as natural or synthetic. Natural dyes were the only ones available until synthetic ones were discovered in the middle of the 19th century.

An example of arashi shibori. The dyed lines are a result of the compression of the fabric in the dye bath.

They were obtained from various vegetable, animal, or mineral sources and take their names from the elements of which they were composed. They are not normally as resistant to exposure to light or washing as the synthetic dyes.

Regarding the synthetic dyes, there is a huge variety – acid, azoic, pigments, etc. The dyes more frequently used by artists and designers are the reactive ones, since they can be used to color a wide range of fabric types without the need for any special machinery to fix them.

Dyeing methods

The most common methods of dyeing fabrics are in hot water and in cold water. Materials resistant to heat are required for the former method, while the latter uses very reactive dyes. With silk, the method of dyeing that is used is carried out in cold water because it is more practical and you do not have to waste time heating the water.

Shibori technique

The shibori technique comes from Japan. As a generic term it covers all the techniques by which fabric is embellished using a reserve instituted by pressure. Because of the multiple ways in which we can tie, gather, sew, or fold material and the diversity of coloring that exists, the results can be more than surprising.

According to legend, shibori was devised by a Japanese man when he noticed what happened when he pushed a piece of paper into a tobacco pipe. He observed that when it was removed and stretched out some interesting stretch marks had been created by the ashes from the burnt tobacco. So then, it is said, he tried to test what happened when he pressed fabric into a dye bath in the same way.

There are many ways of applying the shibori technique, depending on how the fabric is pressured, and the addition of imagination and creativity will produce a wide variety of results. This section will explain a method of shibori that is called arashi, which means a storm, because the lines formed by the fabric after the procedure are reminiscent of a torrential fall of water. This special technique was invented in 1880 by Kanezo Suzuki in Arimatsu. From then on, the Japanese became some of the greatest exponents of arashi shibori and came to create more than 100 different patterns.

Karla de Ketelaere, from Belgium, is a major, internationally recognized artist working with the shibori technique. She took up decorative fabric painting professionally in 1984, although, following family tradition, she began as a little girl. Karla has developed many ideas in fabric art, utilizing, in particular, her personal experience with the decorative traditions of Africa and Asia.

In 1987 she settled in Spain, where she taught a large number of courses while working specifically with the batik and shibori techniques. Today she is one of the few fabric artists to combine both processes.

Karla has chosen the subject for the following step by step, which demonstrates one of the 100 arashi shibori patterns, because she considers it to be very simple but at the same time satisfying. It is carried out using floss silk, to show the reactions of another type of silk. Remember that floss silk is made from short fibers. It is a somewhat thicker fabric whose texture is not totally uniform. Shibori can also be applied to other fabrics.

Silk painting for beginners

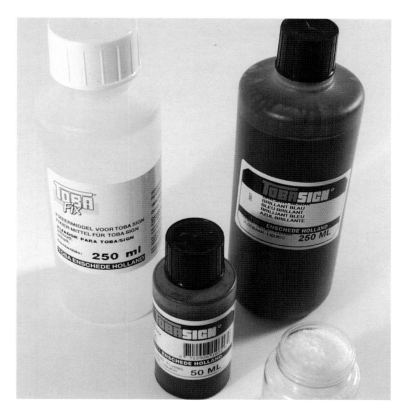

Two different sized bottles of Toba Sign dye — one brilliant blue and the other black — a bottle of fixer, and a jar of salt.

Equipment and materials for shibori

In addition to salt, you need PVC tubing, which you cover with the silk in order to set up a cold dye bath. If you want to use a warm water dye it is important to make sure that a type of tubing that is resistant to heat is used. In Japan this technique used to be carried out over wooden poles up to 13 feet (4 meters) long.

Besides the tubing and the silk you also need: a needle and sewing thread, pins, soft pencil, ruler, rubber bands, washbowl, long, trough–like container for carrying out the dyeing, dyes, cooking salt, and fixative.

The dyes that are used by Karla de Ketelaere are the Toba Sign brand and are reactive. They are ideal for painting and dyeing 100% natural fabrics such as silk, cotton, linen, and wool, and they allow the color to be consolidated in cold water with a liquid fixative or with steam if the technique requires it. Reactive dyes take their name from the fact that they react chemically with the molecules in the fiber to form a covalent bond. This strong bond between the dye and the fiber provides excellent qualities of resistance to washing and exposure to light.

The proportion of fabric and dye–bath varies with each brand of dye, but in the case of the brand used by Karla it is ratio 1:20.

That is:

0.03 oz (1 g) fabric	4 tsp (20 ml) of water

For example:

4 oz (100 g) fabric	3^1/$_2$ pints (2000 ml/2 liters) water
2 oz (50 g) fabric	1^3/$_4$ (1000 ml/1 liter) water

The amounts of Toba Sign dye, salt, and Toba Fix fixer that will be added to the bath are:

Toba Sign Dye	2 fl oz (50 ml) water
Salt	2 fl oz (50 ml) water
Toba Fix fixative	1 fl oz (25 ml) water

So the correlation is as follows:

FABRIC	WATER	TOBA SIGN	SALT	TOBA FIX
4 oz (100 g)	3^1/$_2$ pints (2000 ml)	3^1/$_2$ fl oz (100 ml)	4 oz (100 g)	2 fl oz (50 ml)
7 oz (200 g)	7 pints (4000 ml)	7 fl oz (200 ml)	7 oz (200 g)	3^1/$_2$ fl oz (100 ml)

7 Step by step
GUIDED SALT EFFECTS

1. Two PVC tubes of different diameters that will allow us to dye the floss silk in cold water. It is important to measure the circumference of the PVC pipe with which you are going to work in order to determine the correct width of silk that will cover it.

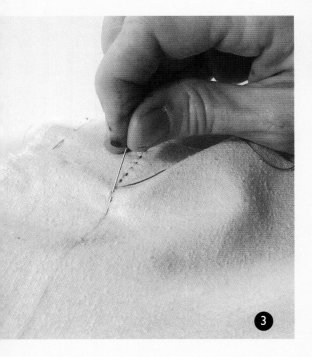

2. Once the measurement of the chosen tube has been neatly marked with a pin, fold the material in half.

3. Using a soft pencil and a ruler, draw a straight line where you have marked the exact measurement of the tube with pins and then begin sewing.

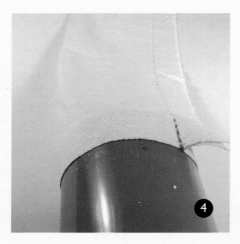

4. Sew one part and check that the silk covers the PVC tube perfectly. If it does, carry on sewing to the end. In this example, a Gütermann dtex 1000 (3) 100% polyester thread was used to sew the silk. The thread should be strong because the silk has to fit the tube tightly.

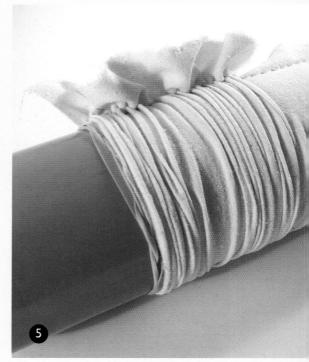

5. Slide the fabric over the tube and check that the sewing is correct.

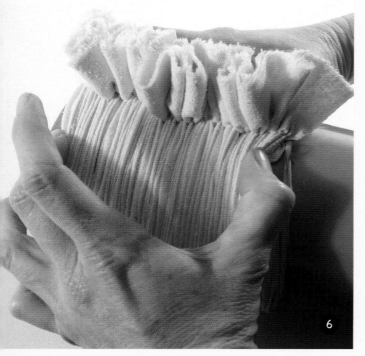

6. By compressing the silk that covers the tube, you are beginning to apply the shibori in its true sense, which, in this case, in order to make an arashi, is done by firmly pressing the fabric together with the hands. Then, so that this pressure is not lost, tie the ends with rubber bands that will wedge the silk together.

7. Before pouring the measures of salt and dye into the container where we are going to do the dyeing, put the fabric that is compressed on the tube into water so that all the silk will be equally wet. In this way the color penetrates in a uniform manner.

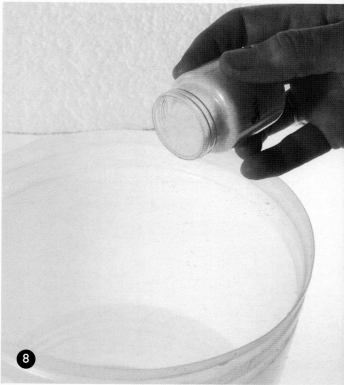

8. Add the salt. This acts as an electrolyte that reduces the solubility of the dye and so creates more uniform coloring, since the dye will be absorbed through the fibers at a constant rate instead of all at once.

9. Pour in the amount of dye that you require to match the weight of the fabric and the quantity of water that will be used to dye the silk, according to the previously given proportions. Check that the salt and the dye are mixed well together.

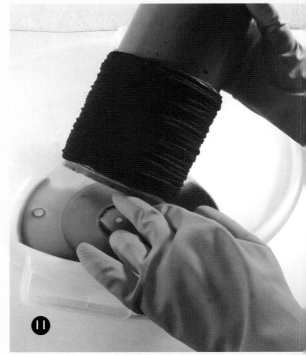

10. Once the bath is ready and the silk has been compressed on the tube, place it in the container full of dark blue dye (a mix of brilliant blue and black). The dye contains reactive substances that allow the pigment to penetrate the fabric easily, although it is also important to keep stirring it during the dyeing process, which in this case will last for about 30 minutes.

11. Once the 30 minutes have passed you should remove the tube covered with the floss silk, while adding the fixative (Toba Fix here) to the bath. Stir it and put the tube back in the bath. Continue stirring for another hour.

12. After an hour remove the tube with the fabric from the bath, rinse it while it is still in place on the tube, and then remove it.

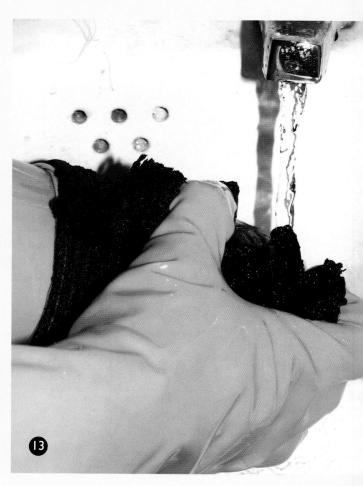

13. Once the fabric has been removed from the tube, rinse it again thoroughly in the washbowl with water from the faucet (tap) to remove the remains of the dye that are always left in the folds.

14. Carry on rinsing the scarf in a container full of water.

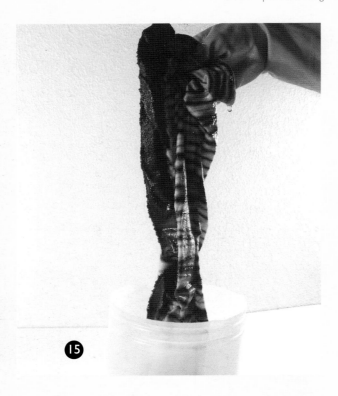

15

15. Stretch the fabric to wring out the water and then wait for it to dry. It is advisable to iron the fabric while it is still damp.

16. This is the finished result of the arashi shibori applied to the floss silk. The edge of the material seems to be completely covered in dye and the lines are a result of the fabric being compressed, indicating that the dye has penetrated more in the areas on the outside.

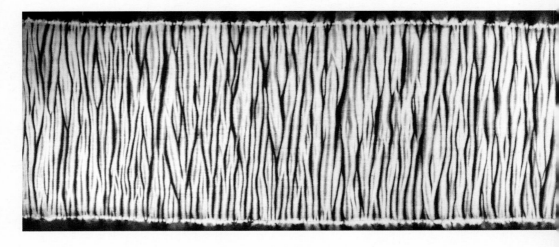

17. An example of arashi shibori, this time on a piece of silk that had been previously painted with the same dyes using the sugar technique. The magic of this technique lies in the huge variety of shapes that you can achieve by dyeing using compression and pressure.

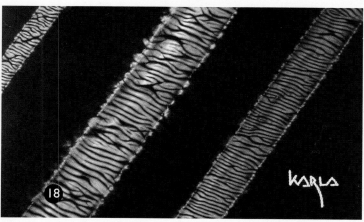

18. Another example from Karla de Ketelaere, made using this same system but with more sewing: a finished product that converts the fabric into a delightful table covering.

Hint

Remember that the more the fabric is compressed, the finer the lines will be. They will be wider when less pressure is applied.

4.2. Batik

Introduction

The name of this technique comes from the Javanese word *ambatik*, which means drawing and writing. It was not until the first decades of the 16th century that travelers coming from the island of Java made this, the original process of decoratively dyeing material, known in Europe. The batik technique used by the natives of Java made it possible to achieve ornamental effects of great beauty. Nonetheless, more than three centuries passed before this technique was incorporated into European craftsmanship.

According to ancient writers, batik clothing was used only by the aristocracy, especially by ladies, who had time at their disposal to dye material because they had servants who looked after the domestic chores. Meanwhile, the working classes spun the cloth for their clothes.

So it was that the Javanese developed and perfected their aesthetic sense through batik and managed to make, and continue making, true works of art on fabric. The first pieces of work showed a particular preference for stylized drawings of multicolored butterflies, birds of paradise, and indigenous plants and flowers. But they also knew how to bring these drawings together harmoniously to form a wonderful decorated surface.

In batik, the drawing is made with wax on white material, so it is more of a resist technique, because the dyes do not penetrate the parts covered by the wax. When the fabrics are dyed in a color bath the designs are preserved, so the process must be repeated for each color that you wish to use as a dye.

The typical cracks and grooves that are produced in the wax when the fabric is manipulated contribute to the composition, as some of the dye penetrates through them. Thus very fine colored lines are formed that constitute one of the characteristics of the technique – the so-called crackle. However, an excess of different colored lines should be avoided, as this would give the design a restless feel. When dealing with multicolored dyes, it is better for the darkest lines to provide the crackle effect. To achieve it, it is important to avoid putting pressure on the material when using light colors, though this must be done with dark shades.

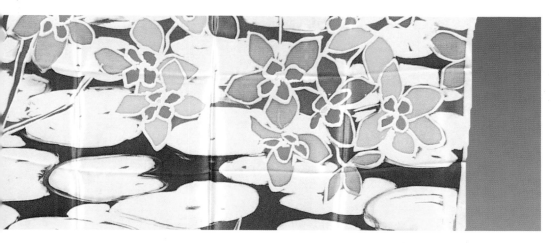

To begin with, you must choose the material, which should be white and with a smooth surface. Either cotton, or natural or artificial silk is best. If you start your experiments in batik with silk you will have the advantage that it does not need any prior treatment and it dyes very uniformly. The choice of material depends on what is to be made with it. For shawls and headscarves it is appropriate to use natural silk, because it has a tight weft and beautiful sheen and also the crackle effect develops more easily, since the fabric is whiter and stands out more. Cotton or linen lend themselves to wall-coverings and tablecloths.

Example: batik on silk

Tina Chueca has dedicated 20 years to professional decorative painting on silk, specifically to batik. She will illustrate this technique with one of her innumerable examples of this specialty.

For the fabric used in this project Tina has selected $^1/_4$ in (5 mm) pongé silk, the fineness of which means it will not need to be taken to the dry-cleaners to remove the wax once it has been fixed.

The design in the example the artist is demonstrating will have an ethnic motif and will be two-toned. In fact, there are no set rules regarding the style of the drawings, since both natural or stylized figures and abstract forms can be featured. What you must keep in mind is that only flat drawings should be made, rather than trying to give any depth to the picture and, when it comes to choosing the design, you should keep in mind the use that will be made of the material.

18 Step by step for the batik technique
PART ONE

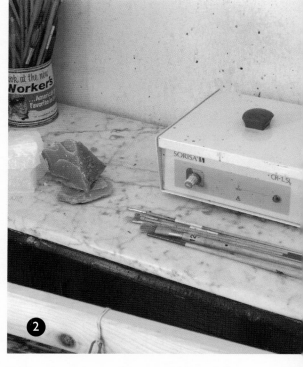

1. Materials needed for making batik: dyes, fixative – in this case the Deka Aktuell brand, which allows the dyeing to be carried out with water that is not too hot – and wax and paraffin, a combination that gives a better crackle effect.

2. To these materials must be added: paint-brushes with which to apply the wax – these should be stiff and either flat or well rounded – and an electric wax heater. When the brush is submerged in the wax and then taken out, lean it on the inside edge of the container so as to remove the excess and prevent it from dripping when it is moved.

3. Another type of applicator for tracing out fine lines of wax is the tjanting, which comes from Indonesia.

4. Once you have selected an appropriate-sized piece of silk, place it in the frame and secure it with the hooks. Prior to this you have drawn the design with a charcoal pencil, which will be erased in the wash.

Hint

It is not necessary to remove the wax that is left on the brush – it can be left there until it is used again. Before using the brush again it only needs to be submerged in hot wax.

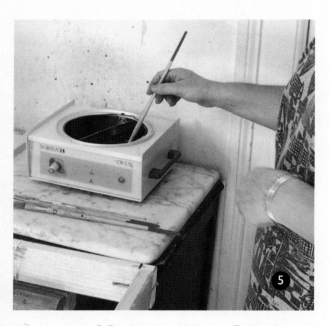

5. Put the wax and the paraffin into the wax heater at the same time. The heater will maintain a temperature of approximately 248°F (120°C). Both substances act as a resistant, and the paraffin also facilitates the crackle effect. The proportion needed to achieve this correctly is 25 oz. (700 g) of paraffin to 10 oz. (300 g) of wax. In this example we have used a very small quantity, in line with the proportion mentioned, because the design is small. The higher the paraffin content, the more the wax is broken up.

6. Begin to trace the wax, following the drawing, with a stiff paintbrush.

7. With the wax and the paraffin at a constant temperature, continue the design on the silk, which must be firmly stretched or it will be impossible to trace the lines correctly.

8. Once the wax has been drawn out on the fabric, it will dry in a short time and you can quickly move to dyeing the scarf.

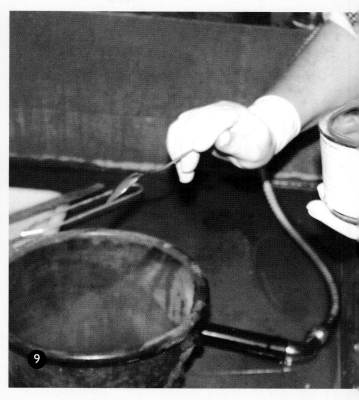

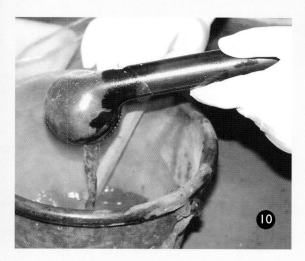

9. Now move on to the dyeing process, for which you will need a container in which to pour the dye, following the proportions given on the envelope. Each wrapper carries the instructions for its use. Normally the relation-ship between the cloth and the amount of dye is 1:30, that is: every 4 oz. (100 g) of material needs a dye bath containing 0.10 oz. (3 g) of dye.

10. In this example, we add 1³/₄ pints (1 liter) water, which must be hot — 86–140°F (30–60°C).

11. It is useful to sieve the dye to remove any impurities and then pour the liquid into the dye-bath you are going to use to dye the scarf. This container should be big enough for the fabric to be stirred inside it and to remain completely covered by the dye.

12. Put the silk in with the wax resistant so that it acquires the color of the dye.

13. It is important to keep stirring the material inside the dye-bath so that it dyes uniformly. The dyeing time is 30–60 minutes. This varies depending on whether you want the fabric to be dyed dark or light, because the darker you wish the dyed fabric to be, the greater should be the concentration of the dye-bath.

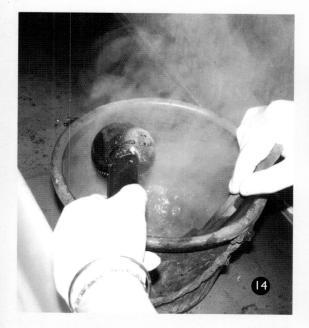

14. Once the silk has been dyed, prepare the fixing solution in the same container in which you mixed the dye. Pour in the percentage of fixative that the manufacturer recommends and add very hot water.

15. Sieve the water with the fixative again and pour the solution into the dye-bath that we have previously emptied of dye solution.

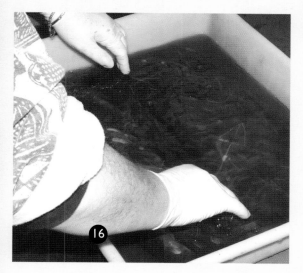

16. Leave the silk in the water and fixative for about 30 minutes, giving it an occasional stir. Afterwards rinse the silk in clear cold water to remove the excess dye.

17. Once the silk has been rinsed, put it in another container, also full of cold water, into which you should pour a little vinegar.

18. Rinse the silk for the last time in this solution because the vinegar fixes the dye better and gives the color more shine.

Hint

For the most effective results, it is better to produce lively colors and gradually dilute them with water or to reduce the dyeing time than to buy light-colored dyes.

Hint

If you plan to continue creating batik it is better to use a professional wax heater rather than a domestic one, because the latter cannot keep wax at a high temperature for so long.

PART TWO

Once the color has been fixed you can iron the silk, after which the result will be a two-tone scarf. But if you want to try the crackle effect, you have to apply wax and dye the piece again. The thin lines that appear in batik creations are one of the most beautiful characteristics of this technique: the cracks that are produced in the wax allow the colorants to seep through during the dyeing process. These fine lines give a great vibrancy to smooth surfaces.

1. Once the scarf has dried naturally, proceed to the second stage. Once again you have to spread wax over the entire surface that does not contain wax and leave the outlines of the drawing without any resistant so that they become highlighted in the new dyeing process.

2. Remember that the wax that you apply to the scarf has to be sufficiently liquid to be able to spread well.

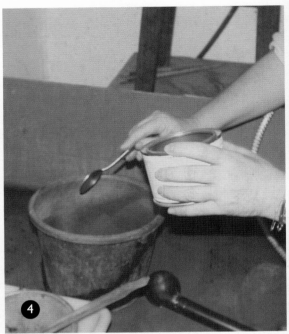

4. Prepare the dye-bath again in the same way as before.

3. Finish "painting" with the wax and wait for it to dry.

5. In this way you can achieve the effects of cracks or grooves in the silk that are so representative of batik.

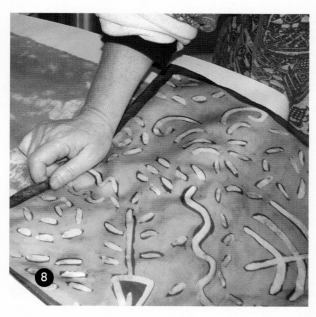

7. To remove the wax, start to iron the scarf. It is advisable to place newspaper underneath to absorb the wax and, on top of this, white or light-colored paper towels so that the ink will not seep through to the scarf.

6. Bathe the crackled scarf in the dye-bath and let the new color impregnate the areas that have not been sealed with wax and the cracks that have been produced by creasing.

8. Use a very hot iron and iron several times on both sides of the fabric, until every trace of wax has been removed from the scarf. If necessary you can see how it disappears and is absorbed by the paper.

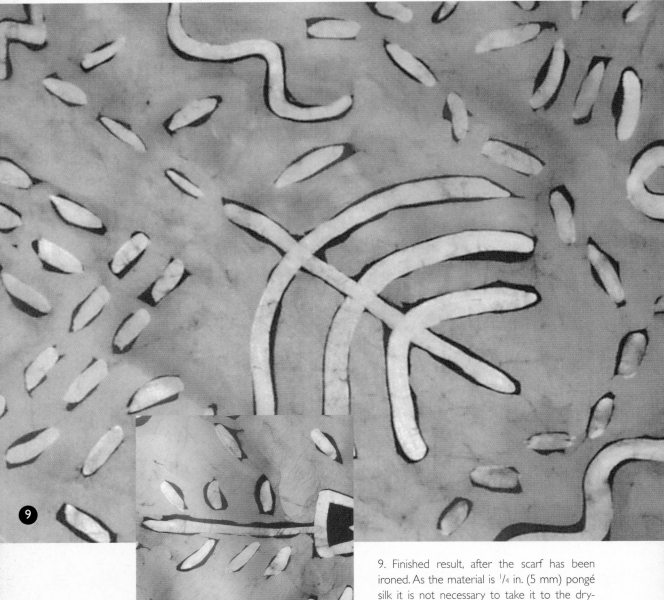

9. Finished result, after the scarf has been ironed. As the material is $^1/_4$ in. (5 mm) pongé silk it is not necessary to take it to the dry-cleaners to remove the wax; simply ironing it is enough. If the material were any thicker it would have be treated professionally.

Detail of the batik example. The white of the silk is a result of the first sealing with wax, while in the second procedure we obtain a darker dye, a color that has not dyed the background because it was sealed with wax at that stage.

10. An example of batik in mauve tones, created by Tina Chaeca.

Detail of another example by the same artist, where the crackle effect can be appreciated in the light-colored areas.

4.3.The fixing process

When you have finished a painting on silk the process cannot yet be considered complete, since you still have to fix the dye on the fabric. In this phase, not only is the dye permanently fixed and bound to the silk, but also the color is enhanced and reveals all its brilliance and intensity. Steaming in order to fix the paint on the silk can be undertaken by a specialist, or else you can do it yourself if you acquire an autoclave (below and page 155). This chapter will demonstrate a simple homemade system with which you can steam-fix samples of silk or small scarves. All the processes result in a fabric of extraordinary smoothness and natural sheen. The added design on the silk, which has recovered its splendor, definitely becomes an integral part of its texture.

Steaming

The machine used by shops that specialize in this sort of fixing and by the silk painting professionals is called an autoclave. This appliance, which functions in various ways according to type, fixes dyes with steam; it consists of a metal tube that can withstand high temperatures, into which the silk is placed to be fixed. Any remains of gutta or wax still remaining on the silk will mostly be removed by this process, but if you want to be completely sure that these substances or antifusant have been removed you can then use the dry-cleaning process. Dry-cleaning removes stiffness and lets the silk recover its naturally soft feel.

Hint

Although some professionals acquire an autoclave from any supplier of silk painting materials, many artists who work with steam-fixing dyes prefer to send fabrics to specialist establishments.

9 Step by step
FIXING AT HOME

Part one

You can construct a homemade steam-fixing system that works in the same way as an autoclave. This method can be used on samples or small pieces of silk.

1. Equipment and materials needed for a homemade steam-fixing system: pressure cooker, adhesive tape, aluminum foil, scissors, piece of clean cotton material, wrapping paper, and special soap for washing silk.

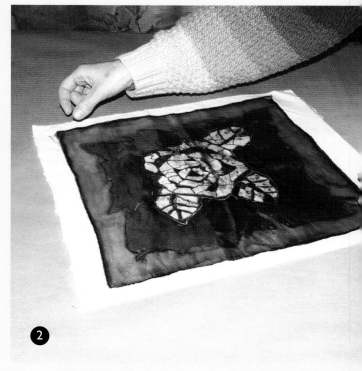

2. First of all, stretch the scarf that you have painted with steam-fix dyes over the cotton material. It is important that one edge of this fabric should remain uncovered by the silk scarf.

3. Roll up both fabrics, trying not to make any creases in the scarf, because these will produce marks during the fixing process.

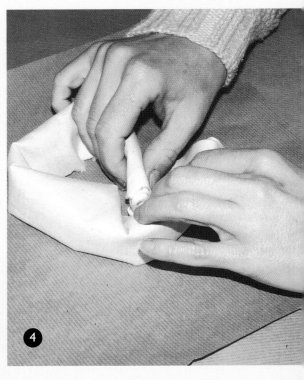

4. Once the pieces of cloth have been rolled up, place them on the wrapping paper as demonstrated here.

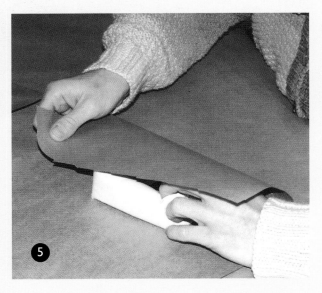

5. Wrap everything in the wrapping paper, but not too tightly, so that the steam can work.

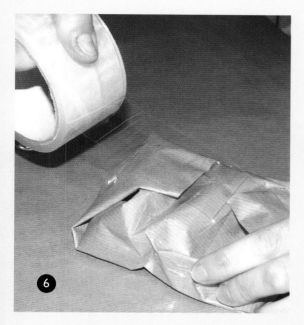

6. Completely seal the entire surface of the package with adhesive tape.

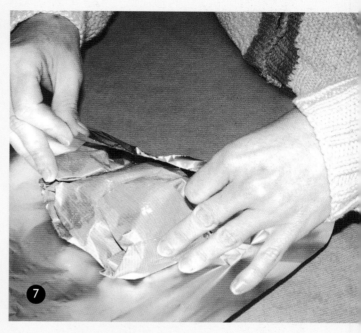

7. Wrap the package again, but this time with aluminum foil, to protect the fabric from water.

8. To be absolutely sure the fabric is sealed, wrap the package up again sideways.

9. The package should not touch the sides of the pressure cooker, so you need an object that keeps it suspended inside the pan. In this case, a steamer accessory is used.

10. Once the package is in place, pour in a reasonable quantity of water (about ½ pint / ¼ liter) and put the pan on the heat. When it reaches maximum temperature, lower the heat and leave it for one or two hours. It is vital that there is always water inside the pan.

When you unwrap the package the wrapping paper will be wet and the silk creased. Spread it out and leave it to settle for at least 48 hours.

Hint

If the silk carries a lot of pigment, for example if it contains very dark colors, if you have been working with salt, or the silk is very thick, then the steaming time should be longer.

PART TWO

Once the silk has been fixed, whether by the home method, an autoclave that you have acquired, or in a specialist establishment, it is essential to clean and iron the fabric to finish off the dye-fixing process and so that the silk can recover its natural brilliance and sheen.

1. Pour the special solution designed for washing silk into a washbowl containing water, in the proportion of 2 fl oz. (50 ml) to 7 pints (4 liters) warm water. While you can use neutral liquid soap, a special solution is recommended for the first wash as it stops the very intense pigments from contaminating the light colors.

2. Pour enough warm water/solution into the washbowl to allow the silk to float and then submerge easily. Continue stirring the fabric again and again so that the special solution removes the excess pigment. You can finish washing when no more color leaks out from the silk.

Once the silk is clean, immediately spread it over an absorbent surface, such as a towel, and start to iron it on the wrong side. This process must be done straightaway, because if you let the silk dry it will be more difficult to remove the creases later on.

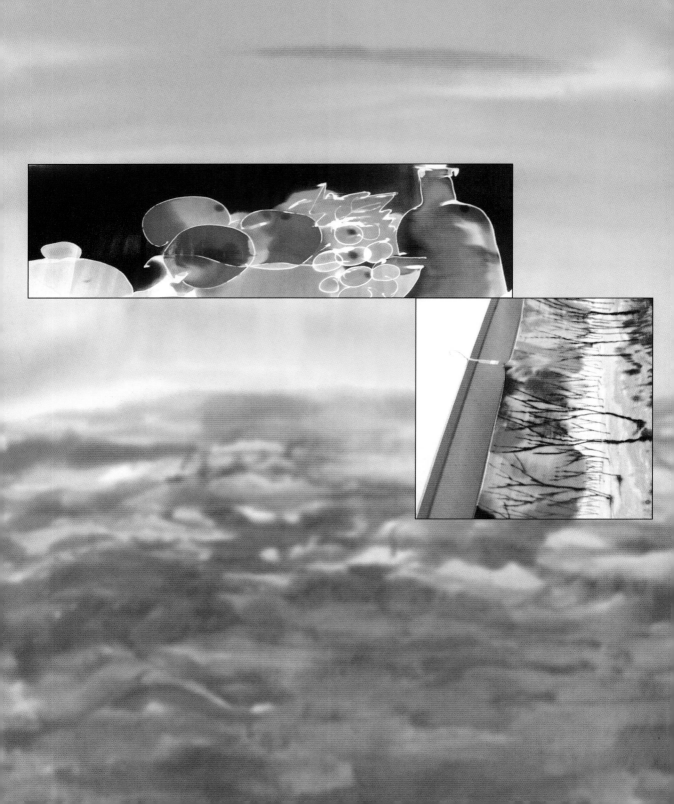

5

Investigating and experimenting

5. Develop ideas by experiment

Once you have allowed yourself to become fascinated by silk after trying out the different effects of the basic and complementary techniques, then it is time to explore, to enjoy experimenting. It is only through this that you will gain experience. This time, as examples, we are going to show four pieces of work completed by the silk painters Jordi Andreu Fresquet and Concha Morgades.

These are four very free and rapid pieces where perhaps it is not the technique that is the most interesting aspect, but the creativity that can be brought to bear on the surface of white silk. Of course, we are not going to pretend that anyone can reach this level with their first attempts at decorative painting on silk. However great the imagination or natural gift we may have for artistic activity, we must first consolidate our understanding of the techniques and know what to use and how to achieve different effects. This means letting ourselves go and waiting for the silk to give us the answers because, as a living material, it acts as an artistic collaborator.

Combining the different techniques

The Catalan painter Jordi Andreu Fresquet normally works with a very loose brushstroke and personal motifs with figurative lines that are transformed into an evocative universe, where the movement and the coloristic atmosphere are the dominant elements.

Although Fresquet is also active as an orthodox painter, some time ago he was seduced by silk and its many possibilities, and since then he has felt the need to experiment with the sensation and vibrancy of color that dyes give to fabric. He will demonstrate over the next few pages some clear examples of the artist's constant dialog with the silk, even to the point where any mistake is converted into a pathway to a new experience.

1

EXERCISE ONE

In this first example Jordi Andreu Fresquet aims to create a natural landscape with bright colors on velvet measuring 5 ft × 14 in. × 0.01 in. (1.53 m × 0.36 m × 1.5 mm). For this he will only use dyes, some of them diluted. This velvet is of double composition, comprising viscose and natural silk.

1. Although the work is going to be very spontaneous, Jordi Andreu has to prepare the dyes that he is going to use, especially the yellow, brown, and reddish tones, and choose silk paintbrushes of different numbers.

2. After doing a few tests with the dyes on pongé silk, he begins to paint yellow and orange strokes in the upper part of the velvet.

3. Jordi Andreu paints small areas of blue color to give the effect of sky through the trees.

4. Once he has made strokes for the trees, he begins to brush along the base of the piece with shades of dark and light brown.

5. He paints the base intermittently to create the effects of light and shadow.

6. Jordi Andreu continues to cover this area with chiaroscuro, leaving a white band in the center of the composition.

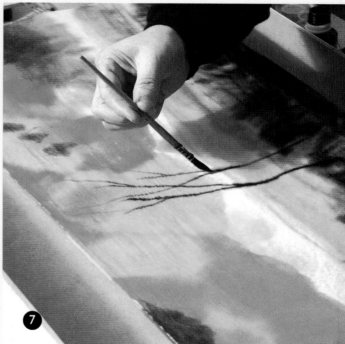

7. With a low-number brush, he begins to paint the trunks and branches of the trees. He brushes from the base upwards and repeats the same operation along the whole landscape.

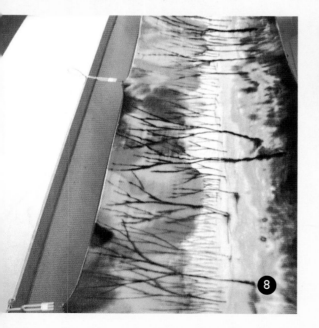

8, Now the painting is almost finished, he only needs to wait and see how the velvet continues the work by spreading the dye. The effect is very colorful and shiny because of the special texture of this type of silk.

2

EXERCISE TWO

Jordi Andreu Fresquet plans to create an atmosphere suggesting a dance on a piece of $\frac{1}{2}$ in. (12 mm) crepe de chine that measures 43×43 in. (1.1×1.1 m). Here, as well as the dyes, he will apply alcohol to create different effects, and add gutta to the outlines of the figures, but without too much concern for whether it follows perfectly the lines of the silhouettes as he wants the forms to be very mobile.

1. Jordi Andreu carefully chooses the dyes and the remaining materials needed for the exercise, and places them in order.

2. Over the crepe de chine he arranges the silhouettes of several human figures that he has already cut from card.

3. Jordi Andreu traces the gutta along the outline of the silhouettes with an applicator to create a barrier against the dyes that he will spread in the background.

4. He begins to paint with ultramarine blue in the upper part and also makes some brushstrokes in violet.

5. As he paints, he dilutes the dyes with water in order to soften the tones.

6. Jordi Andreu adds brushstrokes of intense violet in the upper part of the work to create a greater contrast with the soft shades.

7. He begins to work with the rubbing alcohol, pouring on a few drops to produce interesting effects as the pigment is displaced.

8. Jordi Andreu has painted orange and yellow tones in the central parts and again brushes violets and blues on the base. He continues making loose brushstrokes to help create movement in the image. If a mark needs amendment, Jordi Andreu makes use of it to create another effect, so even an error is beneficial for creating a fresh idea.

3

EXERCISE THREE

This piece of work has been carried out on a piece of ¹/₃ in. (8 mm) pongé, measuring 35 × 35 in. (90 × 90cm). The silk has been divided into three parts with gutta to create three different compositions. The result is a team effort created by Jordi Andreu Fresquet and Concha Morgades, where different techniques are applied in a way that is highly unusual because of their speed, simplicity, and inspiration.

2. He then scatters grains of sea salt onto a landscape depicting a small coastal town.

1. Jordi Andreu begins by drawing the first composition with an invisible ink pen.

3. Jordi Andreu spreads thickener using a stiff paintbrush to create the surfaces of the buildings.

4. Concha Morgades begins to draw another marine landscape next to that of Jordi Andreu with thickener and ultramarine blue dye.

5. Morgades makes a contribution to Fresquet's work by irregular sponging with antifusant to create the effects of the sea and the boats.

6

6. Once the boats have been painted, the image is now finished: a surprising result, given the fast and sculptural work involved.

The antifusant mixed with dyes in the lower part of the coastal town gives the composition interesting effects. Colors are repeated again in the buildings, adding balance to the picture.

The work begun by Concha Morgades represents another way of depicting a marine setting, with strongly contrasting tones. Thickener has been mixed with different shades of blues and violets for the sea, creating an aquatic texture, while the sun and its surroundings have been worked with salt. The result is a scene of waters in motion on a romantic evening.

The final piece of work by both artists consists of another direct painting on silk with the central theme of a still life.

After tracing some basic lines of gutta to outline the shapes, Jordi Andreu paints a few studied splashes of color, achieving an effect of volume in the fruit and the objects surrounding it. When he spreads the dye over the silk, he waits for it to surprise him with its reaction, which is precisely the feature that most delights lovers of painting on silk.

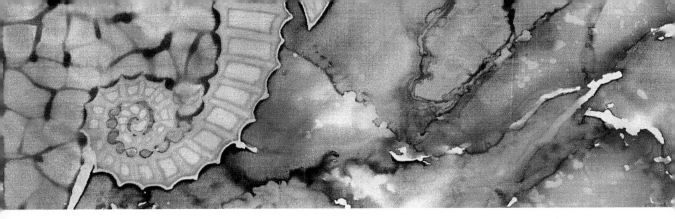

Glossary

Antifusant: A resist that covers the pores of the fabric and allows it to be painted without fear of the dyes easily spreading.

Batik: Deriving from a Javanese word, it denotes the process of blocking the uptake of dye with melted wax.

Essence F: Solvent for products that contain petroleum, such as petrol-based gutta or petrol-based antifusant.

Gutta: Resin gum that contains a milky latex and comes from the tropical *palaquium*. Used as an outliner, blocking the spread of dye.

Iron-fixed dyes: Dyes that can be fixed with heat alone, such as with an iron.

Momme (mm): Japanese unit of measurement that gives the weight of silk. Expressed as mm.

Petit-gris: Name of a special paintbrush for painting on silk. It is made from squirrel hair, which allows a large amount of paint to be absorbed in the upper part and distributes a small amount through its fine point.

Pigments Insoluble coloring substances that have no effect on the material, but can be applied to surfaces through another medium that creates a link between them and the fibers of the fabric.

Print: A design on the surface of a fabric.

Reactive dyes: Dyes capable of reacting with the substratum, in the correct conditions, to create a covalent bond between the dye and the material.

Resist: Substance that stops the dye from settling in the substratum of the areas where it has been applied. The resist can be a mechanical or chemical barrier.

Steam-fixed dyes: Dyes that contain a high concentration of pigment and can only be fixed with the aid of steam.

Thickener A solution of vegetable gums that simultaneously acts as a barrier and gives the color a gelatinous consistency.

Tjanting Tool used to apply wax in the batik process. It consists of a small copper container, which has one or more spouts, with a wooden or bamboo handle.

Warp: Threads that go along the length of a woven fabric.

Weft: Threads that go across a woven fabric.

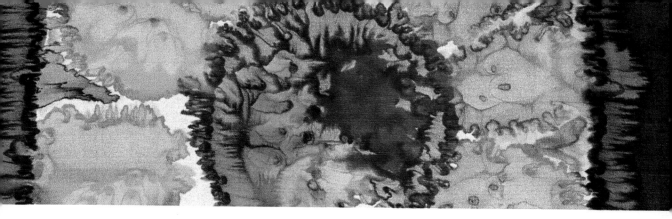

Concha Morgades

The author of this book, Concha Morgades, was born in Barcelona and began to study fine arts in 1970, later going on to specialize in print design, industrial pattern design, and techniques for painting on silk.

Concha began her professional career in Barcelona as a designer in the Indra company in 1976, and four years later started designing prints for the Lluis Batlle studio. At this time she moved on to a new stage in her career, becoming professionally independent and creating the Macchia studio, which was dedicated to print design and jacquard. During this period she began her formative work as a lecturer on prints at the International Feli Institute, an activity that she continued to develop until finally focusing on teaching her great passion, painting on silk.

Concha has continued to work as a stylist for different clothing companies, such as Jacquard Mas Lluch SA. She has also found time to present several exhibitions in, among others, the School of Design in Barcelona, the Textile Museum in Terrassa and the Premia de Mar Textile Museum, receiving various prizes in her specialist field.

Now Concha Morgades dedicates herself exclusively to painting on silk in a professional capacity and to researching the artistic possibilities of this fascinating world, creating unique pieces that are both original and sensual.

746.6   Morgades, Concha
Mor
          Silk painting for
               beginners

1-03-45   14.95